What If

Reflections of My Father's Life:
Sir Jason Winters

Sir Raymond Winters,
KCSJ SOSJ

Printed in the United States of America

First Printing October 2011

ISBN No. 1-885026-16-1

Published by
VINTON PUBLISHING CO.
PO Box 94075
Las Vegas, Nevada 89193

For more information about Sir Jason Winters, visit:

www.sirjasonwinters.com

A Message from the Author

Over the years, there have been many books and many stories told and written about my father, Sir Jason Winters, most of them great. I wanted to write a book about his life and what he meant to me, the adventures he had and what I learned from him. I wanted to protect and ensure the accuracy of his life story—and the creation of the Jason Winters Herbal Tea. So this is my recollection of his life and times. I hope you enjoy reading this book as much as I did writing and living it.

My father had many adventures, interacting with many people in his life. For this book I have simply concentrated on *my* view and what I have learned from him and the effect his life and philosophy had on my life. If anyone feels left out of this rendition—I apologize.

At the end of my book I have included selected chapters from my father's book, *The Sir Jason Winter's Story*, relating to the tea blend he formulated and his cancer, exactly as he wrote it over 30 years ago.

Dedication

It is with great honour that I dedicate this book to my wife, Mia, for her constant support over these 22 years, for allowing me the freedom to travel the world and to write this book, but mostly for her patience, compassion and understanding, and for loving me when I needed it most.

All my love,
Raymond

Thank you,

Noelle and Angela and Angelo,

for your help, encouragement,

and support.

Contents

Love gives naught but itself and takes
    naught but from itself.
Love possesses not nor would it be possessed;
For love is sufficient unto love.

Kahlil Gibran, *The Prophet*

Chapter 1

He Will Be Nothing More Than a Cat Burglar

My father was born in the eye of a rainstorm on September 13, 1930, in a small brick tenement house in Hove, Sussex, England. "It's a boy," the midwife stated calmly. A tall, strange man of few words crossed over to the bed and stared at the newborn. "He will be nothing more than a cat burglar," he said as he turned around and walked out the door. He never spoke to the child or the mother again. That man was my great-grandfather. The baby was my father, Frederick Raymond Jason Winters. We both were born with the same name. I've gone by Raymond all my life, and he did most of his life until he decided to go by the name "Jason Winters" in 1977.

My father felt like an outsider as a child and always had the spirit of an adventurer. In 1940, Adolph Hitler had promised to flatten London. At that time, children were being evacuated from Brighton to the centre of England, and at ten years old, a skinny boy, already over six feet tall, my dad boarded a bus, carrying a small paper bag full of clothes, with an extra pair of shoes dangling around his neck. He would never forget the kiss he got from the man who raised him. It was the only one he would ever receive from the man he called Dad.

In Bristol, Leicestershire, two female teachers walked the streets, dropping off children to a list of families who had volunteered to take care of a child for the duration of the war. The pretty girls and the smaller boys were snatched up first. It wasn't until evening that they were finally able to convince a middle-aged couple, Mr. and Mrs. Freestone, to take the gangly giant. For four months the postman delivered letters, some written on toilet paper, to Jason's parents, pleading, "I must come home; I will walk if I have to. Please don't leave me here." His parents finally conceded and he was put on a train back to London. A German bomb fell on the railway tracks on the way to Euston Station, and in the middle of an air raid, my dad, at ten years old, walked across London by himself all the way to Victoria Station. He was found by a policeman who bought him a cup of tea and a cheese sandwich and brought him to a shelter and then to Victoria Station where he finally had a teary-eyed reunion with his mother, wrought with fear for her son.

At 6 feet 4 inches, Jason had the charisma and charm of Cary Grant. As a teenager, he could be seen running across triangle-shaped factory rooftops like Cary Grant in *To Catch A Thief*, the 1955 Alfred Hitchcock movie. As his grandfather had predicted, like an amateur cat burglar, he and his friends played pranks around town. In 1947, at seventeen years of age, my grandmother and grandfather immigrated to Canada and they left behind the little brick house in Hove forever. Once in Canada, Jason saw a newspaper advertisement for lumberjack jobs. In a lumber camp in Tahsis, British Columbia, with frostbitten hands from below zero degree weather, he worked the worst job, green-chain puller, pulling off a river of sawed tree planks from the constantly flowing conveyor belt. My father then served in the army for three years with the Lord Strathcona's Horse (Royal Canadians) "LdSHRC."

At 23, with $600 in his pocket, Jason decided it was time for a vacation and took a bus to Guaymas, Mexico, where he sat in the sun, swam, fished, drank, and danced with a different beautiful señorita each evening. Almost out of money, he decided to head back to Vancouver. During a layover in Tucson, Arizona, he noticed dozens of people dressed in old western garb, and Native Americans with buckskins and war paint, milling around the Santa Rita Hotel. A well-dressed, elderly man came over to him and demanded that he stand up and turn around. "How much do you weigh? How tall are you? Can you ride a horse?" the man asked. Jason was immediately hired to be the stand-in to do horseback riding, fighting and stunts for Jay Silverheels, the Native American film and TV actor who played Tonto in *The Lone Ranger*. Silverheels was starring in the Universal Studios "B" western, *Walk the Proud Land*, with Audie Murphy, Anne Bancroft, and Patricia Crowley, released in 1956. During scene breaks Jason enjoyed sitting with the Native Americans around the campfire as they drank putrid-smelling tea made from local plants to purify the blood.

My father told me that one night, through the dust of the smoke and flames, a weathered, old Native American looked him straight in the eye, and in a loud, strong voice he said, "You are far from a cat burglar now! Your grandfather wants you to know that he is proud of you and is sorry for the way he acted at your birth." My great-grandfather, Jason's grandfather, had died years earlier. The old Native American went on to explain that he saw a vision of Jason running across something high in the air and made a slanting motion like a triangle, referencing the factory rooftops Jason had run over as a teenager. My father had never spoken a word to the Native American and he never forgot that spiritual encounter around the campfire.

Walk out of This Place Right Now and Marry Me

My father continued making movies and commercials in Hollywood as an actor and stuntman and in 1956 his life became his own Hollywood movie, complete with romance and adventure. Jan was a part-time model working at a vegetable stand in the farmer's market. "What's a beautiful girl like you doing working in a place like this?" he said. "Why don't you just quit this job and come with me right now?" She flashed a smile, exited the booth, and let the swinging door slam shut behind her. She did not look back.

My mom and dad were married a couple of days later. In 1958, Catherine Ann Winters was born in San Diego, California. In 1959, I was born, Frederick Raymond Jason Winters, in Tucson, Arizona. In 1961, my brother, Steven Garth Winters was born in London, England. In 1963, my brother, Mark Alan Winters, was born in Anchorage, Alaska, and in 1965, Christopher Robin Winters was born in Victoria, British Columbia, Canada.

As you can see, my father didn't stay in one place for very long. Of what I can remember and what I've been told while I was growing up, before I was born Dad worked as a lumberjack, an actor, a model, a stuntman, a banker, a private investigator, and founded his own newspaper that he later sold. He also started his own credit control company, was in the army, played the harmonica, wrote music, and wrote two fiction books that were never published.

One book was called "Kill Abraham Jones," about a plot to kidnap the president of the United States and replace him with an imposter. The other was called "War of the Races," about African-American and Caucasian people killing each other in America during the riots in the 1960's. One of Dad's special qualities was that he could do anything he put his mind to. He also wrote a non-

4

fiction book about his canoe trip down the Mackenzie River. I wish that I had copies of his first books, but he only had one original copy of all three books and they disappeared many years later.

Most men lead lives of quiet desperation and go to the grave with the song still in them.

Henry David Thoreau, American author

(1817–1862)

It Will Take a Lot More Than a Storm to Kill Me

Mackenzie River Canoe Expedition 1967

My father was always larger than life. Big, tall, and strong, looking more like Rock Hudson than Cary Grant, he always took the road less traveled. In 1967, I was eight years old when he decided to retrace the canoe trip made by Sir Alexander Mackenzie in 1867 down the Great Mackenzie River from Great Slave Lake to Inuvik, on the Arctic Ocean, to celebrate the Canadian Centennial.

With his friend, Dan Ross, Jason set off on his 45-day journey of tremendous winds, torrential rains, and incessantly biting insects. At one point the men almost starved to death after a storm had badly damaged their canoe. Saved by the Royal Canadian Mounted Police, they were able to repair the canoe and complete the journey and return home. The press, cheering crowds, and Jan, my mom, greeted them, with me and my four brothers and sisters in tow. "It will take a lot more than a storm to kill me, and you can quote me on that," Jason said.

Hot Air Balloon over the Rocky Mountains 1968

Apparently it was the adventure bug that bit my father on that last trip, because only a year later he obtained one of the first balloon licenses ever issued in Canada and announced he was going to be the first man to cross the Canadian Rocky Mountains by hot air balloon. The balloon he purchased was called *Oh Canada*. He also had another balloon called *The Maple Leaf*, and I went up in both many times and thought it was fun but I was still scared for him.

Jason quickly discovered why no one had attempted the trip previously. Updrafts swirled the balloon up to 14,000 feet and then dropped it so low that the gondola scraped the top of the mountains. At 8,000 feet the balloon was free-falling and a freak wind turned the envelope into a sail. It crashed at a speed of 30 mph and my father was knocked unconscious for at least an hour. After he walked for three hours over rough terrain, a man driving a jeep, Ralph Nichols, found him and took him to a hotel in High River where he was treated like royalty. A local seamstress sewed up the balloon and in two days and he was able to complete the trip.

Helium Balloon Attempt—Atlantic Ocean Crossing 1968

"This guy will try anything," stated the press in 1968 as my father prepared to be the first man to cross the Atlantic by helium balloon. My father had replaced the gondola (basket) of the balloon with a small custom-made sailing boat. Thousands gathered to witness the spectacular event as Jason and his partner entered the gondola/boat and prepared for takeoff in the westerly wind from Halifax, Nova Scotia. Amidst a thousand cheers, a nun rushed up and pressed the holy cross into my father's hand, just as the balloon lifted skyward and away. Late that night as they drifted along in complete darkness, the roaring sound of an airplane engine broke the silence. The plane circled, and shined a bright searchlight on the balloon. A voice boomed over the loud speaker, "Good luck," and the plane disappeared into the night. Prime Minister Trudeau had wished them luck.

In the middle of the night the balloon suddenly began to lose altitude rapidly. Jason could hear the sound of the violently crashing waves fast approaching. To slow the descent, they began throwing over all the equipment, including the Marconi radio they had been using to keep in touch with the world. Crashing amid thirty-foot swells they quickly cut the balloon loose to avoid overturning the small boat. Two days later a small yellow sail was spotted by a fishing boat dispatched to search for the men. The mission had failed but my father had cheated death once more and the small boat attached to the balloon that he had designed to replace the usual gondola or basket had saved their lives.

9

New Zealand

"My dad crashes cars into brick walls," I said, standing nervously by my chair. It was my turn to tell the class what my father did for a living and I hated public speaking. There was utter silence in the room. "You are lying, Winters is a liar, he is a liar," a boy behind me teased.

When, I was eleven years old and living in New Zealand my father decided he needed some publicity to promote his new company and convinced the New Zealand government to allow him to test a new seat belt in the Jaguar car by crashing it into a brick wall. Ironically, he also arranged for the stunt to be broadcast by a New Zealand pirate radio station, Radio Hauraki, that broadcast in Auckland from a boat. Radio Hauraki was enmeshed in a fierce battle to obtain a private radio broadcasting license to free the airwaves from the government controlled New Zealand Broadcasting Company (NZBC). I watched my father drive a beautiful new Jaguar up a ramp, fly through the air, and smash through a giant brick wall. He ducked down as bricks crashed through the windshield over his head. He was a little shaky but survived to walk out of that car, larger to me than ever. Why he chose to do a visual stunt on the radio I will never understand.

My teacher said, "That's a really hard one to swallow. You're going to have to prove it, otherwise you are lying." (Foreigners or Yankees, Limeys, Canucks or whatever, had a much harder time in overseas school—I was all of that; we all were.) The next day I brought in my dad's huge scrapbook of newspaper clippings of the Jaguar stunt, as well as the canoe trip down the Mackenzie River and the balloon trips across the Rockies and the Atlantic. The students were totally blown away but they still pestered and hazed me. After all, I was an American-born British-Canadian—with a thick Yankee accent, and I still hated public speaking.

Chapter 2

This Complex Universe

One of my fondest memories of my father was when we were living in Toronto, Canada, and I was about six or seven years old and he had just come home from a five-day commercial shoot. I liked to give my dad presents but I didn't have any money, so I took an old spark plug, wrapped it up with a piece of tape, and gave it to him. "Oh, a spark plug," he said, smiling and picking me up high so my face touched his. He smelled like Aqua Velva after-shave lotion and when he hugged me his face was rough like sandpaper but when my cheek touched his ear it was soft like cotton. I noticed he had a line in his ear just like mine. In his arms I felt safe and the softness of his ear made me feel special, like anything was possible.

From 1969 to 1973 we moved in a loop from Canada to New Zealand, to Australia, to England, then back to Canada, to England again and back to Australia, then finally to Canada. Of course we would always take the long way around the world and visited many countries in Southeast Asia and Europe along the way. In New Zealand, Dad and I would sit in the backyard and look up at the stars in the night sky and he would tell me that God made everything we could see. That there was life out there somewhere and it was okay to dream and to think about things—just things—about the world, time, space, and creation.

In Australia, we would stand on the porch during thunderstorms and watch the lightning strike the ground and watch the cane toads hop up the road. My father loved life, storms, the sea, the mountains, the snow, and the sun. "Even the most brilliant scientists cannot grasp the enormous intelligence that it took to create a simple ant, let alone this complex universe," he would say.

When I was twelve years old and living in Australia, I received a terrible report card from school. The report card said I was "belligerent and rude and didn't listen well." I was short for my age and tended to overcompensate for that. At around the same time my father became curious about Spiritualism. So he and I went to listen to someone talk about it. "This is intriguing," he said, holding my hand as we squeezed our way through the standing-room only service in the Gothic stone cathedral filled with one thousand people.

Sir Arthur Conan Doyle, the creator of Sherlock Holmes, had laid the cornerstone for the church. In 1916, Doyle became the head of a large Spiritualist movement, attempting to prove the existence of spirits from beyond the grave, clairvoyance, and psychic phenomena. Doyle went on to establish churches in many countries, including the United Kingdom, Australia, New Zealand, America, and Canada.

I was hiding behind my father by the back wall of the church when a five-foot tall, old, gray-haired woman with a raspy voice said, "I have one more message and then we are done. I have a message for you, the little boy who got the bad report card." And from the front of this great church she pointed right at me!! I was terrified. My dad pushed me forward to the front into her feeble, shaking hands. Your father will be very famous," she whispered. "He will face a great battle and win; he will endure much pain in his life but he will also change many lives and one day you will exceed him." She also told me I would have lots of girlfriends!!! Wow, I thought, I did not know what she was talking about. At the time I didn't care much about being famous, but I liked it when she told me I would get lots of girls. She told me some other things that I will keep between my father, her and me. Thinking back on it all now, I really wonder how that old lady knew all this would come about so many years before my father got terminal cancer and beat it, or before he even became famous for his story and writing his books.

Anyway, I had a little lump under the skin on my throat about the size of a quarter that the doctor had diagnosed as a fibroid cyst that would have to be removed with an operation. I was terrified as the old woman covered the bump with her trembling fingertips and whispered some kind of rambling prayer. Within three weeks, it had completely dissolved and never returned. If something good could come out of that report card, anything was possible. It was a complex universe, indeed.

Two Dollars to Memorize a Poem

"Fifteen cents if you'll rub my hair for half an hour," he said, as I walked into the living room with his drink: 2 fingers of whisky, Johnny Walker 5 Star (the cheap stuff), 2 ice cubes, and some soda. It was a ritual that had started at 5 cents when I was about seven whenever my dad had a long day at work. It continued up until I was about fifteen and eventually went up to 25 cents, 25 new pence in England, due to inflation. It obviously wasn't about the money. We would watch my dad's favorite TV programs while I happily sat behind him and rubbed his hair.

In 1972, when I was twelve, my father gave me a poem written on bamboo and told me he would give me two dollars if I could memorize it. The poem, *IF*, was written by an Englishman, Rudyard Kipling, born in India in 1865. I hung the poem on my bathroom door and memorized it, originally because I wanted the two dollars. As I read the poem over and over, the words began to mean something to me. The poem is a set of guidelines. They are ideals that are impossible to live up to but good to strive for. It was how my father was trying to lead his life, and his father before him. He was kind of funny in that way. When my dad was a kid, when everyone else was out playing sports, he was home memorizing poems and reading about philosophy. It is amazing to me that all those years ago my dad had the foresight to pick a poem that he was able to translate into his whole life. This section is one of my favorites:

If you can dream—and not make dreams your master;
If you can think—and not make thoughts your aim;
If you can meet with Triumph and Disaster
And treat those two impostors just the same...

My father always stressed that it was okay to dream but that you can't spend your whole life dreaming and you have to set goals to accomplish those dreams. Life is full of ups and downs and you can't dwell on loss, you need to rise above it. The last section of the poem suggests that "IF" you follow the guideposts provided by the poem, "you'll be a Man, my son!" To me, being a man is to do the best that you can and live a good life. If you're a father, be a good dad, and if you are a husband, be a good husband.

In May of 2007, my son, J. Raymond Winters, turned twelve years old. I printed out a copy of the poem off my computer and hung it on his bathroom door. I told him I would buy him a new game for his computer system if he could memorize it: inflation.

My father wasn't all philosophy and poetry. We didn't have a lot of money growing up but we still found ways to have fun. We would go on walks, play rugby, cricket, football (soccer), run and swim. One time, my dad had some of those tan, canvas money bags, given out by banks to transport large deposits, and my brothers and sister and I would cut up newspapers, and stuff the bags full. My dad would chuck them out on the road in front of our house as we hid and peeked through the window. People would drive by, slam on their breaks, pick up the bags, put them into their car, and drive away. For an instant, they would think they were rich. Looking back, I suppose it was not so nice, but at that time, as kids, we thought it was funny. Sometimes the people would drive back and throw the money bags back out the window at us.

A couple of years ago, I decided to carry on the tradition with my kids, Ray, Sarah, and Ashley, while on vacation in Hawaii. We were staying at the Rainbow Tower Hotel right off the beach. My wife, Mia, had just bought me a new eelskin wallet. "Guys need one wallet a year," she would say. I told my family the story about my father and the money bags and Mia said, "No, don't do it. It's not funny."

But my son, Ray, was like, "Yeah, Dad, let's do it." So I folded up little bits of magazine from the room, filled up the wallet fat, and wrapped one of my daughter's purple hair bands around it. We waited until there wasn't anyone walking by and tossed it off the 18th floor balcony. The wallet looked like a dot in the sand.

"Daddy, there is no one there," Ashley said. Then a couple of young guys walked over and circled around as one just snatched it up. I remembered so many years ago doing the same prank with my dad.

The Birds and the Bees

My mom was a great mother to us kids while we were growing up and still is now. She would make our clothes for us, work full time, come home and cook dinner, and do the cleaning. We would help with the chores, though. On school days it would be hectic; Mom had herself and us five kids to get ready too!! "Get up, get up," she would yell—like a sergeant major. We called her that, too, because she treated us kids like we were in the army. With five kids and eight years between us, she had her hands full. But Mom could handle us. She would always say, "I love you." I realize, now that I have kids, how hard it must have been for her in that day and age to have one girl and four boys, all within eight years. My mom worked full time and still raised five kids and she cooked almost every night. We never knew how lucky we were to have her.

When we were a little older, if we were hurt or had a cut or needed emotional support, we would go to my father. He hugged us and kissed us every day. So did Mom, but for me, I always went to my dad because Mom tended to freak out a bit if we were injured. My dad would kiss us boys his entire life. Part of being European, I guess. Oddly the English are known for "Steady on, old chap." So I really don't know where he got that from but it was OK with me. I still kiss my kids every time we say goodbye. One of the better things I got from my father. I like to be affectionate with all of my children, regardless of their gender. I even kiss my son. Although, last year, he was like, "Dad, stop." It was no longer cool to kiss him in front of his friends.

My dad was always the fun one. We could talk to him about current affairs, or how the universe was made, but he couldn't really go there with anything deep or personal, especially about him or his life. Things always stayed on a superficial level. He would tell us, "Don't let people see you squirm, don't let people in, don't talk about the family, and don't let them see you fight with your wife." When I was about eleven years old and my brother, Robin, was about seven, my father nervously tried to explain the birds and the bees. "A boy and a girl are like a hot dog and a bun," he said.

"Well, how does a girl get pregnant?" I asked, knowing full well the real answer.

"Boys have seeds and girls have eggs," he said.

"You mean like a chicken and an egg?" asked Robin.

"Yes," he said and that was the end of that conversation. Boy, was it funny. He was actually embarrassed and nervous—it was fun to see him under the gun like that.

It matters not how strait the gate,
How charged with punishments the scroll,
I am the master of my fate:
I am the captain of my soul.

William Ernest Henley

(1849–1903)

Ray Winters unscathed after his crash. Firemen in the background are ready to counter any petrol explosion in the car.

Sir Jason, New Zealand. Taken moments after he smashed a Jaguar up a ramp and through a brick wall!

Sir Jason, New Zealand

Sir Jason, New Zealand

1

National magazine with Sir Jason's Balloon on the cover circa 1968

THE HALF THAT DIDN'T GET AWAY — All that remains of the Maple Leaf is this 15 foot sailboat in which the balloonists were rescued.

'We Knew We Had No Chance

Whatever goes up must come down.

The trouble was their balloon descended a little ahead of schedule dumping adventurers Mark Winters and Jerry Kostur into the Atlantic Sunday afternoon— less than 24 hours after their dramatic ascent from Hartlens Point.

It would fall free into the ocean and then bounce back into the air, Winters told reporters. After this happened about 30 times, the balloonists decided to pull out the pins and release the 75-foot-high craft.

They landed safely in the Atlantic about 1:30 p.m. in the 15-foot sailing craft that had been attached to the baloon.

The small sail boat was sighted later yesterday afternoon by a Maritime Command Argus anti-submarine aircraft, returning from patrol.

After circling overhead and dropping flares, the aircraft contacted the longliner Karen Dawn, out of Fort Bickerton, requesting Captain Douglas Jack to pick up the two men.

At the time, the Karen Dawn was about 10 miles from the deflated balloonists and eight miles off Sheet Harbour.

She reached Winters and Kostur at 11:30 p.m., about 45 miles east southeast of Hali-

View of boat that saved Sir Jason's Life— Newspaper article after crash and rescue

Balloon being filled with hot air Circa 1967

Sir Jason and Raymond Winters Hot Air Balloon flight circa 1967

2

Newspaper clipping of Sir Jason's route down the Mackenzie River, 1967.

Hoisting a sail.

THE LAST KISS...FOR 32 DAY

...wells were wished yesterday afternoon by Judy and ...left, and Janice and Ray Winter, right, as the two ...ed their journey to follow the canoe wake of Alex-...ckenzie down the river bearing his name. Reports of

their 32-day trip, the f...
175 years ago, were p...
ever they could be re...

...ir Jason saying goodbye to ...eannette Winters, 1967. Before ...aving for the Mackenzie River ...xpedition.

Canoe OGOPOGO Mackenzie River Expedition

3

Sir Jason on the set of western film. Tombstone,
Arizona, circa 1954.

Sir Jason on the set of western film,
circa 1954-1955

4

Raymond Winters, Mr Kazuya Asami, Mr. Yuji Ishikawa, near, English Bay, Vancouver BC Canada 2005, Spreading Sir Jason's ashes.

Mr. Alfian Lau, Sir Jason & Mr. Handy Wang, In Singapore, 2003.

Raymond Winters with Toru Kogure, Yuji Ishikawa, Goro Murakami, Kota Fujii and the staff of EOS Corp, Osaka Japan

Sir Jason, book signing 1990's

Sir Jason and Raymond, on leave from Army, summe 1979

Sir Jason, Singapore Magazine Article, 1999.

Knighthood Ceremony 1985, Lady Jeannette Winters
Rabat, Malta.

Sir Raymond, Sir Gary, Sir Steven.
Knighthood Ceremony. Rabat, Malta, 2010

Baron and Baroness, K. Vella Haber and other members of The Order of St. John.

Baron and Baroness, K. Vella Haber.

Dame Commander, Joyce Darmanin.

9

Goro Murakami, Raymond Winters with Yuji Ishikawa, and Toru Kogure, Good Will Tour, 2009 Kyoto, Japan

Sir Raymond Winters meeting EOS Members. Osaka, Japan 2009

Raymond and Yuji

Kota Fujii & Raymond Winters,
Japan Lecture, 2010

Indonesia Lecture 2010

Lecture, Japan

11

Sir Raymond with
Master Sergio Penh
Seventh degree Brazi
Jiu Jitsu Red and
Black Belt.

Sergio Penha Brazi
Jiu Jitsu Class 20

Sir Jason with Marco and Tony Urera—Manila, Philippines.

Sir Jason and Mr. Yuji Ishikawa, Tokyo, Japan 2004

Sir Jason with Sir Gary Samer
KGSJ, Sydney, Australia.

ERIC WONG TH LEUNG K C SEK SIR JASON WINTERS P L FOO

Sir Jason with Mr., KC Sek, Mr. Eric Wong,
Mr PL Foo, Hong Kong.

Sir Raymond with Sole agents for Indonesia, Mr. Handy Wang & Mr. Alfian Lau

Singapore, Mr. and Ms. Wu

Sir Raymond in Malaysia with Sir Steven Soh, KGSJ and Rowan Soh

Sir Raymond Winters

Chapter 3

Terminal Cancer

It was around my mom's birthday, March of 1977, and I was seventeen years old and we were living in Vancouver. There was a knock at the door of the apartment. I looked through the peephole. "What's Mom doing knocking?" I thought. I opened the door and she immediately started crying.

"Your father has terminal cancer and he's still in the hospital," she said. A wave of utter shock and disbelief ran through me. It was like being in a nightmare—you know, the one where you realize you are dreaming but can't wake up from.

"When is he coming home?" I stammered.

After a painfully long pause, "Eventually," was all Mom could say.

Dad was in a traditional Canadian English style hospital called Prince Mark or Princess Anne, something like that. My sister, brothers and I walked down the cold, sterile, stone hallway that smelled of stale air. This was Canadian socialized medicine in the 1970's. Kind of reminded me of the DMV. The doctor took all of us kids into this little room and said, "Your father is terminal. We will try to save him but you have to get your affairs in order. When you go in and see your dad, don't cry." It was a very cold and emotionless talk from the doctor that has remained with me to this day. That feeling of being so helpless and unable to help my own father overwhelmed me.

Once in the room, we saw that Dad was hooked up to a pump that was sucking up fluid and saliva because he couldn't swallow. He had just endured a long biopsy operation that had left a nine-inch scar on his neck and throat. There were tubes sticking out of him and there was nothing I could do! We all started to cry. Later he would say, "After a lifetime of fighting *God* it took about fifteen seconds to become a Christian." That was when the doctor looked at him and said, "You have terminal cancer and you've got about three months." My dad believed in God, although he never considered himself a religious person. "There are no atheists on the front lines," he would say.

At the age of 46, my father was diagnosed with infiltrating squamous cell carcinoma, cancer of the throat, tonsils, jawbone and tongue. A tumor had grown to the size of a grapefruit and was strangling his carotid artery and was attached to the wall of his jugular vein. The doctor said that the tumor was growing and the tumor would eventually cut off the blood going to or from his brain. There was talk of some operation that would remove an artery from Dad's leg and this would replace the cancer-stricken artery—but even then no guarantee. The doctor also indicated that Dad would have to have a radical neck dissection to remove his tongue, jaw bone, tonsils, and the inside of his throat, if the radiation worked. We were devastated. Cancer affects everyone in the family in some way. To me, it was the end of everything that I loved, I thought.

Dad had been smoking thirty cigarettes a day since he was fourteen years old. I remember a year earlier, he had asthma so bad that he couldn't run anymore or even walk fast and he had to be propped up with pillows so he could sleep. My dad continued to smoke the first couple of weeks after he found out he had cancer. "I'm going to die anyway," he would say. It wasn't like him to be so negative. My dad was diagnosed with cancer after we moved to Vancouver from Australia. When we were living in Australia he had a blockage in his left ear and a giant swelling on his neck. The doctor had said he had surfer's ear. He took some antibiotics and in two months it went away completely. During that time though, I noticed my dad started getting depressed. He began taking a little yellow pill, Valium, just like the Rolling Stone's song, "Mother's Little Helper." In Vancouver, when he began the agreed-upon regimen of cancer treatment, the depression grew worse and the pill-popping increased. He was to receive three cobalt treatments each day for five weeks—1970s-style cobalt radiation treatments of his head and neck. If the swelling went down he would then be rewarded with radical neck dissection surgery. It had to be hard to stay positive under those circumstances.

Don't Worry, I Won't Forget to Die

It was a different time then, in the 1970's. The cancer ward was filled with smoke, as depressed and fearful patients tried to find courage in each glowing cigarette, and comfort in each powdered donut. Doctors were like gods, feared and worshipped for having the power over life and death. My dad didn't buy into any of it and his positive attitude came back with a vengeance. When he was scared, he smoked, so he decided to quit smoking. He would be "the master of his fate." The poem *Invictus*, written by William Ernest Henley in England in 1875, was one of my dad's favorites. Henley had tuberculosis of the bone and had to have his leg amputated beneath his knee when he was 25 years old. He wrote *Invictus*, which is Latin for "unconquerable," from his hospital bed. He became the "master of his soul."

My dad wasn't a quitter. He didn't want his family or fellow patients to think negatively and he wouldn't allow us to even say the word "cancer" or go to the hospital with him. Even as my dad secretly complained to my mom that everything tasted like cardboard, he would tell his friends in the cancer ward that they would get better and "we will all go out to lunch when this is over." The doctor would plead with my mother, "He doesn't act like he's a terminal cancer patient. He won't listen to us. He's having pillow fights and wheelchair fights and races around. You know, you've got to go home and you have to tell him that he's going to die. You have to make arrangements."

The nurses would be furious when they would find my father laughing with his friends down the hall. "Don't you know you have terminal cancer? Don't you realize you should be in bed?"

My father would just smile and say, "Don't worry, I won't forget to die."

When my dad went for cobalt-60 gamma radiation therapy, he was custom-fitted into a white plastic mask covering his face, with three holes in it to attach to the radiation machine. The mask kept his head still so that beams of radiation could be shot from different angles through his head to meet at the centre of the tumor to kill the cancer cells, while reducing damage to the surrounding healthy cells. He would joke that the mask made him look like *The Man With The Iron Mask* by Alexandre Dumas, or the phantom from the 1925 film, *The Phantom of the Opera*. It was no joke though, as his hair began to fall out on one side of his head and his face became red and purple with radiation burns. He began looking into natural products, such as laetrile from apricot kernels, honey, and vitamin E oil to treat his face. Here was a 6' 4" guy whose weight had just dropped from 260+ pounds to 170, wearing a hat with a sash to cover his scar, searching through microfiche in the library with his big hands. Back then, research information was stored in microfiche that you could scroll through on a screen to access all the periodicals on a specific topic.

My dad maintained that positive attitude even as people began to die around him. He watched his friend with whom he had pillow fights become a blind skeleton. He had a large tumor on one side of his face and his eye was sewed up to stop fluid from oozing out of it. After a month of eating pure honey and treating his face with vitamin E oil, my dad had gained back some of the weight, and healed his face completely.

Feeling great, as he was walking down the hall to his meeting with the doctor, a horrible noise jolted him back into reality. A woman on a gurney was screaming, scratching, and dragging her fingernails along the wall as she was being wheeled into the operating room to get her tongue cut out. The anesthetic hadn't taken effect and she knew when she woke up she would never talk again.

In the meeting, the doctor told my dad that the radiation treatments weren't working and he wanted to schedule the surgery as soon as possible. "Don't tell any of the other patients about the natural treatments you used for the radiation. They might think they can cure themselves," the doctor said.

"Will this surgery allow me to live any longer?" my dad asked.

The doctor responded, "Probably not."

My father came back with, "No operation," and walked out the door.

Fighting

The whole time my father was traveling around the world and fighting for his life, searching desperately for anything that might help him, I was in the army. He couldn't afford to support me and I had turned 18, so he had said, "You have one week to get a job or join the Army."

I said I couldn't get a job in a week and he said, "Well, you can join the army," and he signed me up and off I went. I remember the bus pulling away and wondering if I would ever see my dad alive again. I watched as my mother cried and I strained to see them both until the bus had gone too far.

At 18, I was alone and on my way to twelve weeks of boot camp. After completing boot camp at CFB Cornwallis, Nova Scotia, I went to the 3RCHA in Shilo, Manitoba. There, I transferred to my father's old regiment the Lord Strathcona's Horse (Royal Canadians). There I drove a tank, a Ferret Scout Car, an armored personnel carrier (APC) M113, and trucks full of oil and gas. I was the Sergeant Major's driver and my call sign was Three Niner Charlie. Ironically I joined the same regiment as my father.

When I walked in, the Regimental Sergeant Major said, "Winters, I served with your father." He had served with my dad and remembered the name. After my father got out of the army, the regiment went to Korea, where many were killed. Now, battling cancer, my dad had his own Sergeant Major to rely on and he relied on my mother like a rock. They had become super close during his cancer battle and she was always there for him. She traveled everywhere with him; she always had. Deep down they were soul mates, even though they sometimes fought throughout those tough times.

I'm Too Scared to Die

Having lost faith in the medical system, my father set out on a mission to find a natural remedy for his cancer. He began by eating 50 apricot kernels a day until he went to the health food store to find the kernels had been removed from the shelves by Canadian government authorities. Laetrile, a natural substance, is made by extracting amygdaline, also known as B 17, from the soft kernels inside apricot pits. It has been banned in the United States and Canada since 1971, despite numerous claims of its ability to kill cancer cells. Unable to get laetrile treatments in Canada or the United States, my dad traveled to Tijuana, Mexico, where he checked himself into the Contreras Clinic run by Doctor Ernesto Contreras. Founded in 1963, the Contreras Clinic specialized in nutritional and spiritual cancer treatments and is still known today for its successful use of laetrile and enzyme treatment.

Miraculously, after ten days of treatment, the tumor had shrunk to half the size. When my dad returned to Canada the doctors were stunned and expressionless. "God wants us to be healthy, so he gave us everything we need to live long healthy lives," my dad said. "Things that are sweet in the mouth are bitter in the stomach and things that are bitter in the mouth are sweet in the stomach, like apricot kernels," he continued. Deep in disbelief, the doctors still felt my dad should schedule the surgery. My dad had lost all faith in the medical establishment at this point and once again walked out.

Despite laetrile treatments and a strict diet of fruits, vegetables, and vitamins, in about a year the tumor grew back to its original size. My dad felt like he had been given a chance at life only to have it snatched away again. He could no longer fight the depression and prepared to die. Searching for comfort in religious books, he began to notice how frequently herbs were used as medicines in the Bible and other spiritual texts. Hypocrites, Buddha, Krishna, the North American Indians, the Gypsies of

Europe, and the Aborigines all spoke of healing herbs. With a light in his eyes, my dad looked up from his books and declared to my mom, "I have found faith in myself and decided I'm too scared to die." With a newfound strength, his quest to find the healing herbs that God had put on this earth had begun.

This is my recollection of my father's journey and discovery of the tea formula that saved his life.

Tea story

In 1977, my father was diagnosed with terminal cancer, (squamous cell-infiltrating carcinoma).

Once Dad started learning about herbs as medicine, he became excited. He read that the most powerful ancient herb for tumors seemed to come from Asia. No one seemed to know about it and the more difficult this herb became for him to find, the more determined he was to find it. *Buddha called it herbalene.*

When he learned that it was available in Singapore, that's where they went. Dad lost no time in looking for the herb, which was not available in the stores in Singapore. At last he came upon an old lady living a distance from town, who cultivated the herb.

It was in a concentrated liquid form which she sold for a very high price. Usually sold in half-ounce bottles, she was surprised when Dad asked for one pint. She told him it would definitely get rid of his cancer. My father said he held that bottle with great reverence—after all, this is what he was told that that the great Buddha suggested for tumors.

For ten days he took the medicine, and when nothing happened, he doubled the dose. The tumor, although not getting any bigger, stayed the same size exactly. A hurried visit to the old lady brought merely a shrug. She had no idea why it had not worked. She said, "Well, at least it's stopped growing," and that was it. My mom insisted that they buy another pint from her, even though we still had a lot left over.

They left Singapore feeling very low indeed. Dad felt the herbalene did not work, and maybe that was why it didn't. Next destination was Tucson, Arizona.

Years before, my father had been a stunt man and a bit actor in Hollywood. He had made a few films in a place called Old Tucson. He had learned at that time about a tea which most Native Americans drank for health, and that's why he went there. In Arizona he soon located the herb. Once again he heard that this remedy had been passed down through the ages and may prevent or get rid of cancer.

He drank this tea drink five times each day and at the same time my father was still using the Singapore herb as well. He was not getting better.

In Tucson, a nutritionist who learned of his condition told him that in Europe there were many old remedies for different ills, even cancer.

So with five pounds of the Arizona herb and a pint and a half of the Singapore potion they boarded the plane for London. He had already spent most of his cash and was now on credit cards. I remember Dad later saying that was the only time in his life that he ever appreciated credit cards.

While at a clinic in London, Prince Charles, who was visiting a friend entered the room. He began a long conversation with my dad about his interest to integrate orthodox and unorthodox medicine, natural and chemical healing, all under one umbrella, to expand the scope of traditional medicine. He called it Integrated Medicine. "Don't worry, Mr. Winters," the prince said, "Only God can tell you when to die."

Remembering all the references in the bible, Dad contacted the Archbishop of Canterbury, Lord Coggan. Remarkably, he actually got Coggan on the phone. The Archbishop did some research and concluded that there was a good chance the mysterious herb referenced in the Bible was red clover. The Gypsy health drink that is supposed to be good for many things. Chopped up red clover blossoms make a very nice tea, which he started drinking, also at the rate of five glasses each day. This meant that he was busy making tea all day, first with the Singapore herb and the Arizona herb, then red clover.

On the fourth day he became very ill indeed. His legs were shaking and he felt terribly sick. He had to stay in bed. He stopped taking all the herbs and readied himself for death. My little brother was sent home from school because he broke down and started crying. When asked why, he said, "My dad is dying of cancer."

That changed something in my father and as a last resort, he started back on the herbal teas again. One morning, he was at his lowest ebb. He thought, "To heck with it, I'll mix all the herbs together."

"Jason Winters Tea" was born. From the first sip he felt better, really good, like he was going to live. He told me he felt like life was drinking into his body. I had called my mom the next week and when I talked to my dad, he was totally different. It was like night and day. "I am going to live, I am going to survive, I am going to beat this thing, Raymond," he said. Something in the tea formula had given him the spark he needed, the will to live. My father began drinking a gallon of tea a day.

Nine weeks later, the nurse turned white as a ghost as my father's strong, vital 6' 4" frame walked into the hospital to be examined. There was no sign of the cancer. He said the doctors actually looked like they were mad that he hadn't passed away. Rather than admit the possibility that the tea had helped him, they seemed at odds with him. They couldn't fathom that perhaps, just maybe, they didn't know everything and maybe there was something else that God put in this world or in nature that we just didn't know about. My father responded, "Well, thank God I didn't let you cut my throat." He knew the truth and he was now unconquerable. He had won the war and that was all that really mattered. He was alive!!!

Have faith, your darkest day may turn out to be the start of a wonderful life.

Jason Winters

You see, faith is the opposite of doubt, so if you do not have faith then you have doubt. You can no longer rely on anything, because doubt prevails subconsciously in everything you do. Now, constant doubt causes worry—worry causes stress—and stress causes illness and death. Where there is faith there is no fear, where doubt prevails there is always fear. This is a proven, undisputable fact, proven by the great thinkers of the world, and also proven in my own life.

Jason Winters (Perfect Cleanse, 1984)

Chapter 4

Tea for Two

When my father first told me that he thought the herbal tea combination had helped him beat his cancer, I thought he was crazy. It was hard for me to believe that a tea could do anything other than taste good. But as word of my father's recovery spread around town, cancer patients began showing up at his front door. Before long, over 100 people were showing up each day to learn more about his miracle. After six months had passed, he had received more than 10,000 letters.

On leave from the army at Christmas, I came home to a huge crowd outside our little apartment. My dad was busy giving away the tea. He eventually had to start taking donations to keep up with the demand. Around that time, an article came out in the *Toronto Star* about a little girl who drank the tea and survived leukemia, and although my father never made any health claims for the formula, the demand for the tea just exploded. Companies began approaching my father to go into business with him but he wanted to keep it in the family to maintain the quality and integrity. Having just survived terminal cancer, he was happy and still naive.

Money does strange things to people. There was a priest in town who said to my dad, "Take me in as your partner and we will make a million. We can charge fifty dollars for a 4-ounce bag and I can get the hell out of this church." My dad threw him out of the house, mortified by his greed and hypocrisy. Another man my father hadn't even met ran an advertisement in a newspaper saying that the tea had "cured" his brain tumor. At the same time, several companies began selling phony teas claiming to be my dad's formula.

My father never claimed that the tea "cured him of cancer," but that it boosted his immune system, allowing his body to defend itself. He always said he was in remission. In the late 70s, in a report to the British Medical Association after testing the herbal combination, Dr. Ian Pierce wrote, "the herbs are not a cure at all but merely purified the blood to such an extent that a person's natural immune system starts working and the body has a chance to heal itself. These herbs would have the same effect on most illnesses." In the meantime, I went back to the army and my mom and dad took donations to set up shop in the Bahamas. My father wrote his book, *Killing Cancer* in 1980 to set the record and the story straight. *Killing Cancer* is now in 17 languages and millions of copies are in print worldwide. In China there was even a version of his book in comic book form.

When a positive article came out in an American health newsletter about the tea, the orders started flooding in. In the article, there was a PO Box in the Bahamas where you could send payment plus postage to get the tea. The first day there were like 3, then 5, then 7, then 12, then 20, then 50, then 1,000, then 5,000 orders. Then it suddenly stopped. My dad went to the post office to see if there was a problem. The postmaster said, "You're getting more mail than the Shah of Iran!" He wasn't kidding—in January of 1979, during the Iranian revolution, the US-supported Shah of Iran abandoned his throne and took up exile in the Bahamas, waiting to receive permission to be admitted to the United States for medical treatment.

"What are you guys doing? You selling drugs?" the postmaster said.

"We're selling tea," said my dad and the postmaster said, "Oh, by the way, here's your mail," and he opened a door to a whole mailroom filled with about 20 bags of mail and every bag contained about 5,000 orders. My father went from being a broke cancer victim to being wealthy overnight. On October 22, 1979, the Shah of Iran received permission to enter the United States for medical treatment for his malignant lymphoma diagnosed years earlier by French physicians. The controversy over the U.S. support for the deposed leader lead to the Hostage Crisis on November 4, 1979, where 66 Americans were held for 444 days when a group of Iranian revolutionary students took over the American embassy in Tehran. The Shah died a year later.

Think Positive, Positive, Positive

After having served in the army, my dad wanted me to come to the Bahamas and help him with the new business he had started with my mom, Jason Winters Herbaltea Bahamas Ltd. My life in the Bahamas was great. My dad was alive and we were all happy. Those were good days. I stayed there for six months and then we all moved to Las Vegas. I'm not sure why, but my mom was the one who picked Las Vegas for the start of their new company, Nevada Natural Herbs. This later changed to Tri-Sun International. In 1984 we formed Jason Winters International, which is now Sir Jason Winters International.

While I was working for the family business, I was going to college for business and psychology. I quit a couple of times and also worked at a glass store selling windows, as a lifeguard, and selling shoes at Mervyn's. I always went back to the company, even after getting fired. One day, I showed up at 11 o'clock after drinking the night before at a college party. I didn't shave or comb my hair and my dad saw me and said, "You look like you just got up."

I said, "I did just get up," and he said, "You're fired."

I called my mom and she said, "I know you made a mistake. You have to call your father and apologize." I didn't want to apologize but knew I had no choice.

After six months of working selling shoes, I called him and said, "Dad, I love you and I'm sorry"

He said, "That's all I wanted to hear," and he gave me $500. In the 80s it took a long time to make $500 selling shoes, so I was back and I was happy.

Working with my dad always came with one condition. I had to do whatever he wanted. There was no sitting on the fence with him. If you were not on his side then you were against him. When I got into arguments about business with my father there was no winning. It was lose-lose. There was no gray area. It was always black and white. It was his way or the highway. He had beat cancer, he was unstoppable, and he had all the control. "Don't let anyone tell you when you are going to die, for that is up to you, your mind, and your god. Don't let any man run your life. You must always remain in control," he wrote in his book, *In Search of the Perfect Cleanse,* in 1984.

My dad also had no problem running my life. He was confident in everything he did. I remember this time we were at the Desert Inn in Las Vegas, seeing Steve Lawrence and Eydie Gorme do a show and there was this man sitting in the next aisle smoking a cigar. My dad says, "Sir, would you put that cigar out? And the guy goes, "No." So my dad stood up, took the cigar out of the guy's mouth, and put it out in the guy's own drink and said, "You should quit smoking. You're going to get cancer. I did." It is often said that there is nothing worse than a reformed smoker. He was a reformed smoker. He believed that people could control their thoughts. "Thoughts are things, just like when you throw a stone into a pond, the waves ripple," he said. He believed the waves the mind creates had an effect on oneself and other people.

There was a convention my dad and I were attending for the National Health Federation and one of the speakers had just written a not so flattering article about him. In front of 5,000 people, in the middle of this guy's speech, my dad stood up and said, "I'm the 'infamous' Sir Jason Winters and I want to know how you could write those bad things when you don't even know me?"

The guy said, "Well, hold on, Sir Jason. I'll give my speech and then I'll talk to you," and my dad waited patiently for the man to finish his speech. It turned out, my dad happened to be on the same airplane flight back with the man. After talking at length with my dad during the trip, he realized he was wrong. He recanted the whole story and wrote a two-page article about how wonderful my father was. That is how my dad rolled. "Think positive, positive, positive, all the time," he said. You create your own reality. "Learn from your mistakes and always do your best no matter how little or big your job is." Dad used to sweep the floor in the warehouse.

"Why do you sweep the floor when you own the company?" I asked one day.

"Because it makes me happy," he responded. My dad was never too big to sweep the floor or help someone in need, usually a perfect stranger. He filled his days with helping people, never wanting recognition.

Faith Can Move Mountains

My dad loved to say, "I didn't start to live until I had cancer." I do believe he thought it was the best thing to have happened to him. He felt that before the cancer, he lived life how he wanted, without a purpose. After getting cancer he said, "It was like God reached down and shook me and said, 'I didn't put you down here just to have fun. I put you down here for a reason.'" The success of the tea and my father's message spread all over the world. My dad became famous as testimonial after testimonial rolled in, as more and more people discovered the tea's benefits. Millions of people know of Sir Jason or have used Jason Winters formulas worldwide.

In 1995 my dad received a letter from HRH the Prince of Wales, surprised to hear that my father was still alive. Prince Charles told him how he had established a Foundation for Integrated Medicine in England, "with the object of integrating the best of clinical with the best of complementary medicine, or traditional medicine." He told my father, "Go out into the world and be a peacemaker," and my dad did just that. He embarked on a world tour, promoting and researching alternative medicine and medicinal herbs. He wanted to find a way alternative medicine could work together and create a harmonious relationship with traditional allopathic medicine.

There were years when I hardly saw him. He was always in some far-off place, talking with the local native people, while keeping an open mind about plants and the traditional therapies the local people knew and used. He went on to become President of the Federation of Integrated Medicine and was given a certificate of meritorious service from the United States Congress in 1992 for his work. My dad also received the Medal of Honor in Madrid and awards from around the world.

In 1985, Jason Winters became Sir Jason Winters, when he was knighted in Malta as a Knight of Grace of The Sovereign Order of Saint John. He also held additional posts within the order—Knight of Grace, Knight Grand Cross of Grace, Grand Samaritan of The Order. Her Majesty Queen Elizabeth is the head of the British order and Nelson Mandela is also a Knight of the order, as are many other influential and famous people. This was one of the proudest days of my dad's life. The Knights of Saint John wore a red cross during the Crusades and among other duties, were responsible for helping people wounded in battle. The honor was bestowed upon my dad for creating his herbal tea formula and helping so many people in the integrated health field. The Knight of Grace is one of the highest honors you can receive in that order.

Another one of my dad's favorite things to say was, "There is no such thing as false hope, for hope is faith and faith can move mountains." He believed you have to have hope in everything. Every day when you get up you must have hope. Hope that you're going to have a good day and really that's just faith, faith that everything will go well. With hope and faith you can do anything."

It is no wonder Tony Robbins asked my father to write the introduction to his first book, *Unlimited Power*, in 1986. Tony Robbins has made his career on the idea that personal and professional success and fulfillment in life can be achieved by changing our thoughts and beliefs and taking action. Tony Robbins said, "Beliefs have the power to create and the power to destroy. Human beings have the awesome ability to take any experience of their lives and create a meaning that disempowers them or one that can literally save their lives." My father embodied everything Robbins was talking about. In the introduction to *Unlimited Power,* my father describes how Robbins helped my dad free himself from his childhood fear of public speaking by turning fear into power.

"We have people lying in bed, with their minds dwelling on death. Their doctors have told them that they have cancer, and they are so upset that their bodies are full of stress. Now, if my lifetime phobia can be eliminated in one hour, Tony's methods should also be made available to all of those who are suffering any kind of illness—emotional, mental, or physical. They, too, can be released from their fears, stress, and anxieties."

In the introduction, my dad went on to say, "I'm sure that *Unlimited Power* will be a bestseller because it goes far beyond eliminating fears to teaching you what triggers any form of human behavior. By mastering the information in this book, you will be in complete control of your mind and body; thus, your life."

The book was a bestseller and it catapulted Tony Robbins's career.

Chapter 5

Like Father, Like Son

My dad had become a celebrity, so other famous people were always trying to contact him. I found this sometimes to be disingenuous. They only wanted to be associated with him because he was famous. I would go overseas and people would be super nice because I was Jason Winters' son. They would call me "Sir Jason Junior." I came to understand the rules of the game and just accepted it. When I started training in martial arts, the rules of the game became even more apparent. Like business, fighting is a psychological game. It is 90% mental and it is very much an art form and a sport. We are all sometimes impostors in business. I keep my hair short and have to wear a grey business suit, but underneath I will always be me.

Life is funny and has a way of coming back on you. As a kid, we spent some time in Prince George, BC, Canada. As an adult, years later, I was driving my car back to Prince George and I saw that this wealthy guy, that used to pick on me in school, was digging a ditch in the middle of nowhere by the side of the road. As I stopped for the flag person in the construction area, the guy said, "Ray, is that you?" I said,

"Yeah, it's Ray."

"I am Bob; you remember me?" he said.

I said, "No, I don't remember you." But oh, I remembered him all right.

"Remember, you used to work at McDonald's and we used to mess with you all the time?"

I said, "No I don't remember that but I did work at McDonald's, thanks, okay." I drove off and left him in the dust. He and his friends had tormented many others and me in school so I was glad to see him there in the fields. I know it's wrong—but it's the little things that make one happy!!!

It took me until I was about 40 years old to really stand up to my father. It was hard to be confident around him but I knew part of the future of Sir Jason Winters Tea was going to be on the Internet and he just didn't see it. I started preparing to market the tea over the Internet, quietly hoping he wouldn't notice, but he just pushed me and pushed me, and eventually forced me to take a stand. He could see I was up to something and kept asking me what I was doing and I finally told him. "Oh, no," he said and we had a huge fight.

I looked up at him, into his face and said, "What do you mean, no?"

He said, "You're going to run the company first my way and you're doing that Internet on your own time."

I said no. It really was the first time I ever said no. "I'm going to do this Internet and it's a good thing." He looked at me for a couple of minutes and then smiled and said okay. After that, I went to Japan and gave a speech by myself and for the first time I really felt he respected me.

He actually told me, "You did a good job Raymond, I am proud of you, good work." WOW, those few little words meant the world to me. I always thought I was a disappointment to him. This was 2003 and it had taken that long. I knew my father loved me, as his son, but it was the first time he ever said he was proud of something I had done in business. This small gesture meant everything to me.

Love is Sufficient

Life was great for Sir Jason. People just adored him—maybe it was that he was tall or had that great British accent or that he really knew how to use money to have a good time. To this day I still cannot find what that certain something was that set him apart from most people. But as I remember things about his life, I realize that this difference in the way he thought, and the way he lived his life, probably saved his life many times over. I think a large part of growing up is being able to accept your parents as human beings, fallible and imperfect.

When I was a child my mom and dad were both larger than life, like gods, and they seemed absolutely happy. They never yelled, argued, swore, or fought. As I got older I began to realize that they were just people. They had troubles like everyone else. However, they both learned to accept each other for who they were and stuck by each other through thick and thin, especially when my dad had cancer. Ironically, that was when they were the closest. My mom traveled the world with him when he was frantically looking for herbs or anything that would help save his life. She started the tea business with him and really ran the company in the beginning. My mom and dad divorced in 1984 after almost 30 years of marriage.

As for me, I've been married to my Mia for over 22 years. It is a good love story. Of course, you have to work at it. This requires a lot of talking and a lot of compromises. My motto is Happy Wife—Happy Life!!!

I think my dad was a true romantic. He was looking for the kind of love he saw in the movies. He dated many women, looking for the perfect one and I feel it had a negative effect on his life. As he grew older, he became more loving, understanding, and open. He was a softer, gentler, more philosophical person and you could get inside easier. He was genuinely interested in how I was and what I wanted out of life and what made me afraid or unhappy. It was not until near the end of his life that he realized the love of his life was actually my mom. My mother was the one person who had remained his friend throughout all the years, the one who moved all over the world with him, and the one who raised five children and endured good and bad times with him. He tried to reconcile with her but it was too late. She had moved on. Who could blame her?

In 2004, 20 years after they had been divorced, my dad called my mom up on the telephone and sang, "Some Enchanted Evening," the hit song from the musical, *South Pacific,* to her. Before he had cancer, he would sing all the time. He had a more innocent, juvenile, childish outlook on life. It took him years to get that back and when he got older he began singing again. The last line of the song is, "Once you have found her, never let her go. Once you have found her, never let her go!" He told my mom that she was the love of his life and he made a big mistake letting her go.

He didn't expect to get her back; he just wanted her to know that he loved her. He said he loved her with every fiber of his being. It wasn't just out of obligation or habit or because they had shared so much together or that she was his ex-wife. Or because she was the mother of his children, and stood by him when he had cancer, helped him start the business, and traveled around the world with him even after their divorce. It was more than that. He finally appreciated my mom for the person she was, inside and out. He told me he loved my mom unconditionally like you love a child.

That's how I feel about my children. Love for your child is not subject to any conditions. No matter what they do, I am still going to love them. In the end that's what my mom and dad had. Despite all the turmoil throughout their marriage and after, they loved each other, unconditionally. Most people can only hope for that.

For life and death are one, even as the river and
the sea are one.

Kahlil Gibran, *The Prophet*
(January 6, 1883–April 10, 1931)

Chapter 6

My Father's Last Day

My dad called me early on Sunday, December 12, 2004, and said he had not felt well all week, and asked me to come over to his house that night. He had just returned from a wonderful PR trip in Japan. The Japanese people loved him and he loved Japan. I thought it was jet lag. "Come shopping with us, Dad, it's Christmas," I said. He didn't want to come because it was Sunday and he was going to Taco Bell for lunch and he loved Taco Bell. Ironic for a man that was a former vegetarian and health food advocate. But Sunday was his day to eat whatever he wanted. I told him I would be over that night after I finished Christmas shopping with Mia. At about 6:30 p.m., we were in the car heading home when my cell phone rang. It was my daughter, Sarah, crying and asking to speak with Mom.

I had a deep feeling of dread. Mia talked to her and then said, "Pull the car over because I have to tell you something." I pulled the car over and Mia said, "Your father has collapsed and the ambulance is going to take him to the hospital." I thought, "Okay, this is bad news but not that bad, because you know, everything is going to be okay." This was my father, the world traveler, the adventurer, and the cancer survivor. He had just had a doctor's appointment and received a clean bill of health except for a cold he had picked up while traveling overseas that he was taking a prescription for. I dropped Mia off and was at St. Rose Dominican Hospital in ten minutes.

It was a Catholic hospital and modern, only about five years old. I went to emergency and said, "I'm Raymond Winters," and the nurse immediately said, "Oh, come right this way." Then I knew it was bad. Normally they make you wait at least a little bit. Then I saw my best friend, David—how he had arrived so quickly still remains a mystery to me. I assume Mia called him. He asked what was happening. I said I did not know, as I just had walked in. I remember thinking how like Mia to call David. It was good to see him there.

What a terrible walk through the waiting room and down the sterile smelling hallway. I remember thinking my life was probably going to change but hoping everything might still turn out to be good. I was still hoping. A string of Christmas lights blinked on and off as I made my way through the hallways. My adrenaline magnified the sounds echoing through the hallway. A young girl was crying to her mom while trying to pass a kidney stone. A boy who broke his foot playing soccer was getting a metal plate put on it. A girl had been bitten by a spider. I couldn't help thinking, "Wow, if it could only be that easy."

As I peered into the doorway, green, red, and blue lights from the monitors blinked, beeped, and clicked away, casting an eerie glow over my dad struggling for life. Four nurses were over him with one doctor pumping his chest. Something was sticking outside of his neck, and lines were attached on top of his hand, to his wrist, and fingers. He was asking for me, saying, "Raymond, what's happening? What's happening?" His voice sounded scared and concerned. That startled me and at the same time I had empathy for my father. I felt sorry for him, and me. I felt helpless. There was nothing I could do.

His brown eyes looked blue and dull, staring up at the ceiling. I think he knew I was there but when they finally let me near him he was quiet and still and his eyes were open, then shut. In the struggle to save his life, his hospital gown had opened up. The nurses quickly covered him up while trying to save his life. In the midst of all of the turmoil I said, "Dad, can you hear me?" There was no response. "Fifteen cents to rub my hair for half an hour?" I heard him say to that little boy in my mind. I touched his head and rubbed his hair like I had done so many times when I was a boy and said, "I love you, Dad." Why I had that thought and at that time still escapes me.

By now my father's heart had slowed and there was no brain activity but the nurses continued to administer CPR. I was told my dad's heart was beating only once every six seconds so he wasn't getting enough oxygen to the brain. He had suffered respiratory arrest and his brain had died. "But I heard him ask for me on my way in and I see something moving on the machines," I said.

"There was a cascade of events, a chain of events," the doctor said. "We're keeping him alive. We're doing that now. Do you want us to keep on trying to save him?" the doctor said. I thought to myself—what an odd question.

"Well, yeah," I said. I still had hope even then. "This can't be happening," I thought.

About then I remember seeing Mia for the first time at the hospital. She took one look at me and although we were still 50 feet apart she knew it was bad. I recall how wonderful it felt to have her there, with me and at that point in time and I realized how much I loved her. It was one of those moments that you might have once or twice in your life, if you're lucky.

Looking down at my father, I had an overwhelming feeling of sadness, and pain. I could not help but think, I was watching my father die, my dad, an irreplaceable man. A person that I worked with for 30 years, who raised me, taught me everything I know. I remember my mom came in and just cried. She stayed for a bit and then went out to find the rest of the family. How odd, I remember thinking, that we were together again, Mom, Dad and me, the family, but this was not the happy reunion I had envisioned.

Through the tears in my eyes, I saw a tall blond man walk into the room. It was my friend and my father's trusted doctor,

Scott, my dad's ear, nose, and throat specialist. I later found out that my best friend, Dave, had called him. On a Sunday night, Scott had dropped everything to be there. He had a profoundly concerned look on his face. Scott glanced down at the chart and looked over at the machines. He stood there for a moment, I guess, just trying to gather himself. He finally asked me how I was holding up. I mumbled something and then I could see it in his face.

"Ray, your dad's gone," he said. "Everything that made Sir Jason...Sir Jason...is gone."

"No, Scott," I said. "I can see he is breathing."

"No," Scott said. "We're keeping him alive with those machines and if we unplug them, he's 100% going to die; his brain is already dead, Ray. I know this is a really tough call, Raymond, but you and I both know he has a do not resuscitate."

I said, "I know, Scott, but I can't tell them to turn the machine off. Can you tell them?"

He replied, "I can't do it. You have to do it, Ray! This is your father we're talking about."

"When they unplug him, what's going to happen?" I asked.

"He might struggle for a few breaths or he might just pass," Scott whispered.

A wave of grief and panic overtook me. I looked down at my father and for the first time in my life he looked old. In my eyes he had always projected this vital energy but lying there I could see how the years had worn on him, how time had played its evil trick. He was a person, a real human being, and his body had had enough. I thought about it for what seemed an eternity. Could I live with myself if I did what he wanted me to do? After all he had done for me? Was this the right thing to do? Had the doctors had enough time to try to save him? I wondered, how much time is the correct amount when the brain is already dead? After all, it had only been what seemed a couple of hours. I wondered if his spirit was still in his body. I looked again at the monitor relaying brain function. Still nothing.... Then I mumbled, "Okay, you can unplug him." I knew my dad would not want to linger between life and death, being kept quasi-alive by machines. I justified to myself: his brain was dead....

I leaned over near his face and quietly told my dad I loved him and said goodbye. I asked the nurses if he could still hear me and they said yes. I think they just said it to make me feel better but it didn't matter. Still, I hoped that he would breathe on his own and he would be OK. When they turned off the machine and took the tube out of his mouth, he struggled and took a couple of breaths. Then it was over. A nurse turned the lights out. In the dim green light from the still monitors, I touched his head and he was still warm. I asked if I could stay until he got cold, maybe I would see his spirit leave, or some kind of sign or symbol. Really I just wanted to stay. I just sat there, holding his hand, and thinking about his life. I thought about how much I would miss him and if I was a good son? Had I done everything that I could? I felt the worst feeling I've ever had in my life, a feeling beyond loss, beyond everything. I can only say to anyone that has suffered this loss—I understand.

My mind wandered and I saw myself as a little boy in Sherwood Forest, England, pretending to be Robin Hood, with our bows and arrows, and Dad was the Sheriff of Nottingham. I thought about how much I would miss him and everything that he was. I remembered the softness of his ear. How he loved thunderstorms, the sea, and sunsets. I thought about all the times he told me that death is not the end but the beginning, and that life here on earth exists in just a "blink of an eye." The fun we all had living all over the world. How we were a close family in those early days. How he beat terminal cancer in his 40s, how he helped change complementary medicine, the countless lives he touched, the thousands he changed, and how much he loved life. How happy he looked as I introduced Mia as my fiancée, and when he first saw Ashley, Sarah and RayRay as newborns. Then I thought about me, and how it hurt to see him *die*. I wondered where he was now? What's it all about? Was his life all for nothing? I thought about all that in less than a second.

The Red Cross

I didn't want to let go of my dad's hand. It slowly got cold. It was like touching a mannequin, but it felt great, because I knew once I let it go it was over. All the staff had left except for the head nurse, grizzled, and in her 50s, who was hovering around the machines and trying to clean or sort things. She was winding something slowly, like she didn't want to leave the room. Her eyes were shiny and I saw a tear slowly slide down her cheek. All I could think to say was, "Thank you." She must have done her job thousands of times but for some reason my little episode with my dad really affected her. I think it was because I wouldn't let go of his hand. Maybe she could sense how much I loved my father and it made her emotional. Scott said to me later, "Sometimes people don't stay in the room or don't come at all, and the patients often die alone, but every once in a while, you see something wonderful."

Suddenly, another nurse, a bit overweight, with sandy blonde hair, barged into the room, flicked on the lights, and yanked open the curtain. She looked at me still holding my dad's hand and said, "We need this room, it's been an hour."

"Wow," I thought, "One whole hour?" I hope someone is nicer to her when she has her turn, because everyone is going to have their turn. "What do we do now?" I said.

"Well, the rest of your family *finally* (her exact words) showed up," she said. She showed no emotion, was disinterested, unattached, and just wanted me out of the way. I didn't care because I had already lost so much that day. Someone being bitchy wasn't going to change anything. I walked beside my father for the last time as he was wheeled into a small room down the hall.

The room felt like a closet. The whole family was there and they were all crying—my mom, my brothers and sister, except my brother, Robin, who was living in Arizona. It seemed weird to me that we all lived in the same town but I hadn't seen some of them in years. In the chaos of the moment I heard someone ask, "Where's the gold cross? Where's the gold cross?" referring to the one that had been around my father's neck. It was lost in the events of the day I guess.

Mia somehow had found a Catholic priest who asked, "Can I do the last rites or something?" My dad wasn't Catholic but it was a Catholic hospital and Pat and the rest of the family were. I said, sure, and he did it. A grief counselor asked, "Would anyone like to talk?" but everyone just wanted to silent. Hospital staff were coming in and out.

I was standing next to my dad when Mia yelled, "Look, oh my God." We all looked down to see a perfectly formed cross of teardrop-shaped blood drops extending over the floor onto the tip of my sneaker. My dad's arm had fallen off the bed and the blood had probably dripped from the open tube on his hand, down his finger, and onto the floor.

My memory went back again to that time we were kids playing in the forest. I was about eight or nine and we were looking up at my dad as the sunlight peered through the trees, casting dancing shadows on his face. "One day I am going to die, you guys, and if there is any way to come back, I will come back, and if there is any way to leave a sign, I will leave a sign. There is life after death," he said. I'm sure he believed in heaven and in life after death. I too believe in life after death and I think that the cross was some kind of sign from Dad. The odds of the blood forming a perfectly shaped cross were probably a million to one. So I choose to believe it was him and more, it makes me happy.

Modern Medicine

Hundreds of thousands of people die in the United States each year from adverse reactions to prescription drugs. It is an epidemic. My dad was on a low dose high blood pressure medication when he caught a cold overseas. His regular doctor was out of town, and my dad had a cough for two weeks, and had a radio show coming up, so he got a prescription cough suppressant from another doctor. Unfortunately, I don't know what the name of the medicine was but I feel it could have interacted with his high blood pressure medication. He had been taking the cough medicine for seven days. Four days before he died, he almost fell over at the office. I told him it could be from the new prescription medicine he had started taking some days earlier, but he was determined to get rid of his cough, and continued taking it. I feel the medicine most likely built up in his system to an unsafe level and lowered his blood pressure to the point where his heart was beating once every six seconds, causing respiratory arrest.

After he died, I asked the hospital to give him an autopsy and they said, "Oh no, we don't do an autopsy if they die in the hospital." One doctor called another doctor and they called another doctor and they asked me what he was taking and I told them about the high blood pressure medicine and the prescription cough suppressant. There was no autopsy. I thought the whole thing was odd. At the time it was hard for me to think of anything clearly. I just wanted it all to go away.

My dad never liked taking prescription drugs, or any kind of drug for that matter, but he did believe in complementary medicine, so he wasn't completely against it. With that said, I must point out that Sir Jason was never against the FDA. He always said the FDA was very important. He did take the high blood pressure medicine and had taken Valium when he was depressed. It was ironic that he survived cancer, and may have died from a prescription drug interaction, after having spent his entire life with one goal, to encourage western medicine and natural medicine to work together. Today it is called complementary medicine and this was his mission late in life. He was also lobbying Congress for a National Drug Interaction database. Many Americans go to the pharmacy and get a prescription, and then if they don't feel it working properly, they go to another doctor and to another pharmacy and get a different prescription, and then they take both prescriptions, not knowing that the two could potentially interact.

When my father died, he was working towards a national computerized database where all prescriptions would be logged so that pharmacists would be able to spot potential interactions and stop the prescription from being filled. He was also a pioneer in complementary or integrated medicine and wanted to get all the healing arts working together, including natural medicine, western medicine, Chinese medicine and others, in unison, for the benefit of the patient. Working with Prince Charles and The Foundation for Integrated Medicine and as the President of The World Federation of Integrated Medicine, he was happy that hospitals were established in Vancouver, Canada, and England, founded on those principles. When the Native Americans were using shrubs and plants to cure people, the medicine man, shaman, elder—or whatever label you want to use—had no motivation to lie. He didn't need to get a boat or a new car or house. He just knew the plant or herb would help his people. This knowledge and information had been tried and tested and handed down through many generations of shamans or medicine men.

In America, many people are brainwashed by prescription drug advertisements on television, radio, newspapers, and magazines. My father traveled all over the world, to Borneo, to Tibet, to Nepal, China, Malaysia, Singapore, Europe, the

Philippines, Indonesia, to Afghanistan, and to Pakistan for tried and proven methods of natural treatments, some thousands of years old. He would say, "what if?" What if…some native person in the Amazon forest whose family had been practicing natural medicine for thousands of years knew more than we do about the nature of plants? Why don't we just try it? He liked to say, "What if you can make a difference? What if you can change the world? What if you can take a stand? What if? That's all it would take." The pharmaceutical argument has been deflected to be about safety and double blind studies—I think it's about money and power. The power to control our lives and our freedom of choice.

Chapter 7

I am Totally Alone

The first day I went back to the office after my father's passing, I asked Angelo, my brother-in-law, to come with me. He was my rock. He had been working with me for ten years. Dad liked Angelo, and when he liked you, he would do silly little things to let you know it. For example, one day we sent Angelo on an errand so Sir Jason could sneak into Angelo's office, which was meticulously clean and orderly, and turn everything upside down—his light, computer monitor, desk, pictures and chair, just to watch his reaction!

Another time, Dad saw that Angelo had a crazy black wig on from some Halloween pictures and he asked Angelo for it. This was an odd request, as Sir Jason was about to leave for a Southeast Asia trip—Manila, Singapore, Kuala Lumpur, and Indonesia. Angelo gave Dad the wig and that was that. Two weeks later, we got a postcard. Dad is at a lecture meeting and he is wearing the wig and looking silly in front of about 2500 people. He took the time to take the picture and put it on a postcard and send it to Angelo in Las Vegas. Angelo taped that postcard to the inside cupboard door in the office. He forgot about it.

It was a week or so after my dad's death and Angelo and I paused at the front door. I had brought Angelo to the office for moral support. He put his key in the door and we entered the darkened office. Angelo opened the cupboard and saw the postcard. He cried immediately. Some rock. When we switched on the light, it further illuminated the dozens of pictures of my father and his products, and his books in 17 languages. A lifetime of work spent helping people. He was everywhere. We stayed for about 45 minutes. My father used to say, "If the office ever gets too much, just leave. Just go out and have a walk around the park." We did just that and decided to work from home for a few days. I eventually had to go back to work, and I did, but not that day.

Some time later, it just hit me. I sat there in the office, surrounded by pictures, awards, and memories of my father; it seemed as if for the first time in my life, I was totally alone. I felt I was surrounded with emptiness and pain. Sadness reached into the very center of my soul. I was alone. It felt cold and kind of scary. He was gone and he was never coming back. I could never call him and tell him what was on my mind or ask him, "What should I do? Or how about lunch?" I was alone in the world. I could only draw on those things he had taught me and how he lived life. I had to make big decisions on my own. He wasn't away in Asia or someplace else. He was dead. That's pretty final. That is when some people find God, but my dad dying took away my faith.

One of this life's greatest truths is that we are not guaranteed tomorrow—tomorrow does not yet exist. There is only right now. This time—this exact point in time—is all we are guaranteed. Tomorrow is not a certainty for any of us.

As I drifted through my life, after a time it dawned on me, I was now 46 years old, about the same age my father was when he got cancer. I didn't believe in anything and nothing made me happy anymore. Nothing seemed to matter. I had the same feeling about going to work and not going to work. Going to the dentist to get a root canal was just like going out to a nice restaurant to eat sushi. There was no difference to me. I didn't care about anything. "We're all going to die anyway. Why should I improve myself? Why should I continue? Why get up? Why go on?" I thought. My mind was always racing and it made me anxious. I couldn't concentrate on what I wanted. I would try to pick up a glass and my thoughts would race from colors, to birds, to the ocean, and I couldn't remember simple things, like if I had brushed my teeth or where my keys were, did I lock the door? I didn't realize what was happening to me. I was blind to my own reflection in the mirror.

When I was on tour in Japan I broke down sobbing about nothing and I realized that not dealing with my father's death had to be affecting me. I had pushed everything that I thought about my dad away into little pigeonholes. This was something I learned from him and my British upbringing. I just put it away because I didn't want to deal with it. I knew this kind of emotional suppression could lead to stress, a nervous breakdown, health problems, and potentially cancer, if left unchecked.

At this point I had already been running the company for many years and we had been experiencing much growth and success. There were many challenges relating to the business along the way, but we always overcame them. Now this was the biggest challenge of them all. I was under tremendous pressure to continue the success of the company on my own, go to Japan and do lecture tours and meet our people world-wide. That would mean yearly trips to Japan, Australia, Singapore, Indonesia, Korea, the Philippines and so on. I would now be the Face of the world-wide companies my father and I built. It would be my plan, but also following my father's vision, and I knew I needed to get help first in dealing with my father's passing to do so.

I didn't even want to go to Krav Maga, my favorite sport at the time. I was very good at hiding how I felt, and mostly, I didn't realize anything was wrong. I was numb and unaware that I had checked out. Once back in the States, Mia knew right away that something was wrong with me, and she was relentless in her goal to get me to go see someone—of course I resisted every step of the way—*everyone else had a problem—not me!!!* Mia was unrelenting and I finally gave up fighting her and went to see someone. Mia saved my life. I was diagnosed as being depressed, so I started to see someone. I didn't open up to her for six months and she just took it. I would go there and create things to say just to avoid letting her in. "How was your day? Good, how about yours? What did you do today? How are you feeling? Great, How about you?" On the inside, I was dying.

Thinking back, the only time I ever saw my father cry was when his sister died. No one bothered to call my father about it until a week after the funeral, when we were in the middle of signing a big agreement with a company in Malaysia. My father got the call at the office. When the agent from Malaysia saw a tear in my father's eye, he said he was going to sign the agreement because he saw Sir Jason was a good man because he cried. My dad never called his family or went to see them. He just dealt with it quietly on his own. It was rare to see him express his innermost emotions openly. He kept a wall up.

Even after smashing a car through a brick wall to test seat belts in New Zealand, he was never able to break through his own walls. I had never even seen him squirm and that was the one time I saw him cry. So, I guess I never learned how to deal with loss. I didn't know what to do when he died and after. Or what I was supposed to do. I never saw anyone grieve. My kids know that I am emotional. When I was dropping my son Ray off for the first day of high school, he was staring at me for a long time, and I said, "What are you looking at, Buddy?"

He said, "Like, I'm just trying to figure out how long it'll take you to cry, Daddy, because I know you will." He was right and I still get emotional that first time I drop him off for school every autumn. Thankfully, the girls drive themselves now.

I Surrender

I was going through some of Dad's books at the office when I came across *The Prophet*, by Kahlil Gibran. Years earlier, Dad had underlined parts for me to read, never mentioning it to me. I guess he just hoped or knew I would find the book. He even wrote little side notes, like, "Ray read this part!!!" or "You'll like this one...."

> Only when you drink from the river of silence
>   shall you indeed sing.
> And when you have reached the mountaintop,
>   then shall you begin to climb.
> And when the earth shall claim your limbs,
>   then shall you truly dance.
>
>   Kahlil Gibran, *The Prophet*

While reading that book, I began to slowly get my faith and my life back.

Three months later, I went to Japan, and in the ancient town of Kyoto, I had a vivid dream. My dad was standing on top of me and he was pushing on my chest. The next morning, I was telling a friend about it and he suggested I go see this world-famous Japanese psychic. The last time I was in the presence of a psychic, I was a kid with my dad. I didn't necessarily believe in psychics, and I wasn't sure about the matter, but I did it anyway. I for one always hope secretly that maybe somehow I'll get to see Dad again.

I was expecting an old Japanese man, lit by a candle, in a spiritual temple, only to be greeted by a very western-dressed Japanese man, about 6' 1" and thin, wearing a regular green t-shirt and jeans, in his hotel room. He touched my hand and said, "Your father was with you last night. He was pushing you, telling you to carry on. To go on with your life, keep the company going, and to not worry about him, because he is in a happy place." I told the psychic that I could really feel my father pushing down on my chest in the dream, so much so, I was making an impression in the mattress. "Yeah," he said, "he is trying to tell you to get on with your life." He also told me that my father had a Native American medicine man for a spirit guide and he would always be a strong presence in my life and keep me safe. This startled me because I don't know if I believe in spirit guides but I don't discount it either. However, I choose not to believe in certain practices, like voodoo, because I think it only affects you if you believe in it.

Before I left, the psychic said, "You liked your father's ear." I was blown away by that one. My father's ears were soft, and as a child, and even an adult, I always liked that, without ever really saying anything about it to anyone—it was just something that I noticed. I had never told anyone about that until two years later, at a lecture I gave in Japan when someone asked me, "What is it that you miss most about your dad?" "When he used to hug me, his ear was soft," I had replied.

Reading books like *The Prophet* also inspired me to start writing about my father and that helped me to process my feelings. One morning I woke up and forced myself to take the kids to school. I didn't want to leave the safety of my little room, and I had a fixation that I was going to pass out while driving or that "something terrible would happen" but thankfully, I made it to school and home safely. Later that afternoon, I went to the doctor with Mia by my side, to get the results from my blood tests to see if there was anything wrong with me. "Raymond, physically you're in fantastic shape. Nothing's wrong with you. It's all in here," the doctor said, pointing to his head.

That was when I realized I had to admit that something was wrong with me. Not me physically, but something wrong with what makes me Raymond. Something was wrong with my mind and it scared me enough to make me finally take action. I had been going to my therapist for a while, accomplishing nothing, but this time I decided to try, and I finally surrendered, just as my father had done when he mixed all the herbs together to make the tea, when he was battling cancer all those years ago. He was at his lowest point and had nothing to lose, just as I was. I had put up walls of my own and it was time to break through them. After the first sip of self-knowledge, I began to feel better.

My therapist asked me, "What do you think made you depressed in the first place?" and it just came to me, "I have all these expectations that I'm letting my father down. That it's all on my shoulders." I was under an overwhelming amount of stress I felt from my father, even in death, and had a tremendous weight on my shoulders. I was doing it to myself. My father never put that responsibility on me. He was the one who told me my life is special and I am worth something. He made me feel like I could do anything and anything was possible. But he was gone now. I had to handle this myself. Depression was robbing my soul of the joy I was inherently born with. I was sliding down the long ladder to where there was no light. What an awful place to be, and I knew I had to get out and back to being happy as fast and best as I could.

Over the next six months, I gradually felt better. The giant weight slowly lifted off of me. I started drinking the tea again, started to live again, and had faith again. It wasn't faith in religion I had been searching for, but faith in myself, in my family, and my positive outlook. After that day, I realized that I was going to do great and everything would be okay. I had never lost faith in God; I just couldn't see clearly because I didn't care about anything at the time. That faith had been there all along and always would be.

Ashes to Ashes

Now that I had let go of myself, it was time to let go of how I felt about my father's passing. It was time to think of him in a positive way. It was time for me to realize his life was special and it did count. It was time to celebrate him and move away from the sadness and grief.

My dad was cremated per his wishes and a funeral was held at Palm Mortuary. I had booked a room for 160 people, but 300 people showed up from all over the world, including many friends from Japan, and we ended up having to move into a larger room, that happened to be a Jewish chapel. Father Ren showed up and jokingly said, "It is just like Sir Jason to cause trouble even after passing." My dad believed in many philosophies and that there were many ways to show your love for God. Then Father Ren proceeded to give a talk in the Jewish chapel to a group of Christians and Buddhists and Hindus, just as my father would have liked it. What a great service that was.

All of my life, my father had told me he wanted his ashes released in three places he loved, near English Bay in Vancouver, Canada, in the Bamboo Forest in Kyoto, Japan, and off of Victoria Peak in Hong Kong, China.

My friends, Yuji and Kazya, our business partners from Japan, whom my father and I had known for 15 years, joined me in Canada. Kazya brought the tea to Japan in the late 80s, as well as introducing Sir Jason and me to Yuji. Kazya remains one of my most trusted mentors and advisors. Truly a holy man.

We had lived by English Bay in Vancouver and Stanley Park was his favorite park. It is a traditional, old English-looking park in the middle of the city. I remember going to a restaurant there where we had toast and tea. In the park there was always this little old man who pushed a popcorn cart and we would get popcorn and ice cream. Then we would go to this beach at English Bay, off the beaten path, called Second Beach, where we would swim and play.

Anyway, the mortuary had split up the ashes for me but I had to get a special permit to carry human remains on the airplane. The ashes had been packed in a plastic bag that was inside a little velvet pouch that was inside a beautiful mahogany box. I took the ashes and put the velvet bag in a simple tin can. My friends and I took a walk through the park to Second Beach and looked out over beautiful English Bay. It was a great day. We said a silent prayer to ourselves. "You're finally home," I said. Yuji and Kazya said a Buddhist prayer and said something very thoughtful in Japanese and clapped three times. We all had a sip out of a flask full of Crown Royal whisky in honor of my dad and I sprinkled his ashes out into the sea. We sat there for a bit. I was pretty somber and I reflected about my dad's life and saw myself as a boy swimming far out into the ocean, as his ashes drifted out to sea.

"For life and death are one, even as the river and the sea are one." –Kahlil Gibran.

In late August of the following year, Yuji, Kazya, Goro, Toru and I met in Japan and went to the Bamboo Forest in the ancient capital of Kyoto. It was hot, about 100 degrees and 80% humidity. We trekked deep into the forest, wearing black suits and ties, to a sacred place. When we arrived at the shrine, I knew it was time to begin my life again. I could feel the life flowing back into my veins as I decided to become a better person from that day forward, to take care of myself, and take care of my family. No more suffering. The Buddhists believe that all life is suffering. If you take away the suffering, you take away the chance to grow. I had done some growing in that last year or so.

In the Bamboo Forest we came upon the spot where Sir Jason's ashes were to be released—a secret spot that only we knew. We all said a prayer led by Yuji and Kazya. The experience

73

was wonderfully spiritual. The five of us share a special bond just because of our experience there. A warm breeze whistled through the bamboo as I opened the little velvet pouch and spread his ashes into the wind.

The last place my dad wanted his ashes spread was at Victoria Peak in Hong Kong, China. That is where the 1955 romance movie, *Love Is A Many Splendored Thing*, starring William Holden, was filmed. It was about a British writer, which my dad was, who falls in love with a beautiful Eurasian doctor. He's a war correspondent during the Korean War and they fall in love. When he dies, she poignantly releases his ashes on Victoria Peak. I haven't been to Victoria Peak yet, but am planning a trip soon and am hoping that Kazya and Yuji meet me there. I think the place had a special meaning for my dad, because he was looking for love all of his life. The song, "Love Is A Many Splendored Thing," was originally written for the movie. I can't help but think of him whenever I hear it.

Chapter 8

I Can Make a Difference

Before my first speech after my father's death, I was terrified. Our Japanese agents had booked a big tour and my father always said that our future was in Japan and Asia. The stress I felt to continue my father's work was overwhelming. I had just had what I thought was a horrible TV recording session in the USA and had visions of my public relations people saying, "Raymond, you suck. You are going to *die* overseas."

The radio shows were even scarier because I couldn't use a set speech and people were always calling in to derail you. My PR company gave me a book called *Present Like a Pro*, and it saved me on that trip. It said not to make political jokes and to never talk about religion or politics. In fact, you shouldn't make jokes at all because they might not come across as well in other cultures. I took my dad's speech from his already scheduled upcoming tour, a tour that he would never go on, and combined that with some of my own words and another dozen speeches he had given, and hoped for the best. They loved it. I was finally applying what my father had taught me over the years. My dad was thinking outside the box before they even had that saying.

When I went overseas by myself, I took the time to get to know the people. I would walk around in my shorts and t-shirt and experience their culture. My confidence increased as my speeches improved and I was off and running. Once back in the US, I began to find balance in my life and my work. I found that I was more productive if I took time for recovery and recharging. My normal day became dropping the kids off at school, going to the office, going to Jiu Jitsu, and then going back to work. Or going swimming and then returning to work. As my father would say, "If the office gets too busy, then just go. Trust your intuition." Not only had my faith in myself returned, so had my positive attitude. I wanted to be successful and I was. My father was gone but his words were always with me. At an awards banquet in Tokyo honoring Kazya and Yuji, as well as two other humanitarians, with the "The Sir Jason Winters Memorial Award of Excellence," I gave one of my favorite speeches.

Speech from Japan

Thank you for that wonderful and very kind introduction. It is truly a great honor for me to be here tonight. I am happy to be in Japan representing Sir Jason Winters.

Before we get started, I want to thank my father for having the foresight and courage not to die and to fight terminal cancer and formulate the tea all those years ago. Because of his determination, we are here tonight. Because of the Jason Winters tea and the great positive effect my father's life has had on the world, we are here, doing good things for Japan.

In the USA we have become a nation that relies on pills, and no wonder!! It seems that we are surrounded by negative news wherever we turn. Our can-do attitude has disappeared. Just turn on the TV—the news is always bad: news on the war, on the terrorists, the environment. What we need is some good news.

We have to break that chain. We have to surround ourselves with happy, positive people. Thinking that good things are happening to me and I deserve it. That I create my own good luck by my attitude and by the choices I make—that we must be positive, positive, positive, all the time. It is unnatural to be ill; natural to be healthy. People need to hear that there is hope for them that does not come from the pharmacy. That it is ok to try something natural.

Isn't it great that we get to help people? That brings me to those two little words, "what if?" You may ask yourself these questions:
What if I can make a difference?
What if I can help people?

What if I change my attitude?
What If?

I would now like to share with you something my father taught
me...
Something very simple yet has had an enormous impact on my life.

He taught me this:
MY LIFE IS IMPORTANT,
I DO HAVE A CHOICE.
I CAN MAKE A DIFFERENCE, IN THIS WORLD
I AM SPECIAL AND MY LIFE HAS MEANING.

Some may ask, how does this relate to me? Well, in order to be
successful in business or any venture, you have to be successful in
your own life.
You must realize that you can accomplish great things!!
You must have faith in yourself.

I believe that the faith he had is what saved him when he had
terminal cancer and that same inner faith is what set him apart
from everyone else.

I remember early one morning in Singapore, we were walking
around a beautiful lake, surrounded by trees with yellow flowers
on them. There were office workers dressed in gold gis, doing Tai
Chi. All I could think of was I was tired and missing home, and
Dad seemed to be right at home. I asked him, "Why is it that
wherever we are in the world, you always seem so happy?" He
said, "I know where my heart lives," and he pointed to himself. I
didn't say anything because I did not know what he meant. He

78

said, "Wherever I am in the world, Raymond, I am at home." No matter where he was, that was the best place to be.

I realize my father was not an ordinary man. You have heard from the speakers before me tonight—how he changed many lives, or how the tea changed their lives and how he made a difference in this world. Now it is up to us to continue making a difference.

If you think that one person can't change the world in a big way, then just try to change it in a lot of little ways.

That is how I intend to spend the rest of my life, continuing my father's work, making a difference one person at a time.

Thank you for being here and please remember the words of the remarkable man who brought us all here tonight...

YOUR LIFE IS IMPORTANT,
YOU CAN MAKE A DIFFERENCE,
YOU ARE SPECIAL,
AND YOUR LIFE HAS MEANING.

O Me! O Life!

O me! O life!... of the questions of these recurring;
Of the endless trains of the faithless—of cities fill'd with
the foolish;
Of myself forever reproaching myself, (for who more
foolish than I, and who more faithless?)
Of eyes that vainly crave the light—of the objects mean—
of the struggle ever renew'd;
Of the poor results of all—of the plodding and sordid
crowds I see around me;
Of the empty and useless years of the rest—with the rest
me intertwined; The question,
O me! so sad, recurring—What good amid these, O me, O
life?

Answer.

That you are here—that life exists, and identity;
That the powerful play goes on, and you will contribute a
verse.

Walt Whitman

Chapter 9

Jiu Jitsu

I have tried many sports in my life—judo, lifting weights, racquetball, running, swimming, surfing, scuba diving, kayaking, and golf. They are all okay but then I discovered martial arts. First, Judo, then Krav Maga, and for the last 5 years I have been a member of a Brazilian Jiu Jitsu club, Sergio Penha Brazilian Jiu Jitsu. Brazilian Jiu Jitsu is more than just a sport; for me it is a way of life. Even when I am traveling around the world on business, I sometimes stop in at BJJ schools to train. Martial arts helped me to deal with the feelings of low self-esteem I felt early on, living under my father's shadow. From training I learned that hard work and pain can be a positive thing. When I'm training, I often think of my father when he was battling cancer and how he endured all those radiation treatments and he never complained to us. He always remained positive, at least to us kids, and always said that he would beat terminal cancer—and he did.

The kind of thinking my father instilled in me helps me to keep going during training when everything in me wants to quit. When I first started learning Brazilian Jiu Jitsu, everything hurt. I got tapped out a thousand times and I never knew if or when I was going to get choked out. Slowly I learned how to roll, what to do, and what not to do. But somehow Jiu Jitsu means more to me than just rolling and winning tournaments—Jiu Jitsu has changed my life!!! Many people are drawn to Brazilian Jiu Jitsu, but only a lucky few can really hack it. We've become almost fanatical about Jiu Jitsu, always wanting to learn more!! My father readily supported me being in martial arts and he would say, "Nothing comes easy and it doesn't matter what you're doing, just do it to the best of your ability and always try." I have to work at Jiu Jitsu every day. I must show up and try hard in order to succeed. I believe this philosophy is how my father beat his cancer, and using it, I beat depression, and became more successful in business. I believe that winning in martial arts and really, in life, is 90% mental. When competing, some guys lose before they even get onto the mat. I've taken this knowledge that I learned through the years of training and listening to Sergio's philosophy with me into the business world and it has helped me succeed in business.

I've learned not to judge people on how they look but to try to understand them better based on how they act. When competing, some guys are big and strong, but when they get into the ring, they turn into a lump of Jell-O. You can do anything you want with them because they can't take the pressure. When you are competing, it is just you and him. When I lose a match, I never give excuses —my foot hurts, he cheated, I'm tired or so on. If I win, I try to act like I've been there before and say "good job" or "nice roll" to my opponent. If I lose, I congratulate the opponent. Sometimes I ask what I did wrong, if I do not know. Whether I win or lose, Sergio always congratulates the opponent and/or the teacher, or says good job. Sergio leads by example and I've always admired that about him. That is how to instruct your students, by example.

My dad never complained or made up excuses when he failed and I don't do it in my life. I am always learning something new and in Jiu Jitsu I will never be good enough to quit. Some people underestimate me because I'm not a flamboyant type of Jiu Jitsu player. I don't look like I'm good or tough.

I remember there was this one tournament where Sergio, now a Red Black Belt, and one of the best Jiu Jitsu players in the world, overheard a competitor from Arizona asking whose name he drew. The guy from Arizona said, "Ray Winters." Just then, his instructor pointed to me and said, "Well, that's him over there." Then he looked back at Mr. Arizona and said, "Look how big you are. You are going to kick his ass," referring to me. I was standing right there with Sergio, and when I heard the instructor say that, it really made me mad. I scored 18 points by taking his back, going for submissions, and basically dominating him in the match. Sergio went to help someone else from our school who was fighting at the same time as me, and that's when I submitted him, and made him tap out. My first sub in a match!! He commented that I did well and he was surprised.

When I stopped doing Krav Maga after my father passed away, I knew I needed help. Once I got over being depressed, I regained my faith in myself and in life, and felt like I could do anything. I remember my father saying, "Hope is faith, and faith can move mountains," and that's exactly what I had—I had hope and faith again.

About a year later, when I was at the Pan American games, representing my club for the first time in my age and weight division, and all these people were watching, I was nervous. It was so bad that when I walked across the mat, I could see the outline of my foot in sweat. I thought to myself, "Go out there and do your best."

Right before the match Sergio said, "Listen to me—don't look at me, just listen," although it became difficult to listen when he was all the way at the opposite side of the mat and at the same time some guy was trying to choke, arm bar, sweep, mount, throw, and basically do anything he could to win, combined with the noise from the crowd and it was a wild and intense match—I won!!

I have learned a lot from Sergio in these last five years. Not just about Jiu Jitsu, but about a way to live your life. I know now that if you give it your all, for every second of the fight, and if you don't give up, even if you lose, you still win. That is if you can truthfully say you really tried 100%. On the other hand, if you give up three quarters of the way through, or with 30 seconds to go, you have to live with that, and I have done both.

Chapter 10

Knighthood

Six months after my father's passing, I received a letter from the Sovereign Order of St. John of Jerusalem in Malta that I was to be officially knighted, as my father had been 20 years earlier, in 1985. However I would have to wait five years for my investiture ceremony. That was to be held in Malta, in February 2010. I couldn't help but think, "Do I deserve this honor?" All I did was follow in my father's footsteps, continue his work, his story, and his philosophy. But, I knew, he wanted this for me. I believe he would tell me I was good enough. I was proud to become a knight of the same order as my father and of Nelson Mandela. My father loved Mandela and one of his favorite quotes of Mandela's sums up both of our accomplishments.

> I learned that courage was not the absence of fear, but the triumph over it. The brave man is not he who does not feel afraid, but he who conquers that fear.

The experience in Malta was like a dream. In a 16th century chapel, Baron K. Vella Haber, the same man who knighted my father, now 96 years old, knighted me. Before the ceremony began he leaned over me and whispered in my ear, "I am happy to meet you. I know your father is proud of you." Then in a breathtaking ceremony, I recited the vows of a knight and was invested in the order my father so loved and supported. Mia sobbed through most of the ceremony. I remember kneeling down and I was touched on both shoulders with a sword and asked to arise Sir Frederick Raymond Jason Winters, Knight Commander Order of St. John. I was awarded my father's posts in the Order and became part of a worldwide and ancient order of knights that is 962 years old.

After the ceremony we were treated to a beautiful dinner at the Casa Bernard, a historic 16th century villa of a Maltese noble family. We had a great time, in our uncomfortable formal clothes, mixing it up with the owners of the house, and the other members of the order. I asked myself, "What does it mean to be a knight, a Sir?" Well, it means nothing if you do not live it in your everyday life. To be a knight of Malta is to live by a code, not just words on paper, but to aspire to do good everyday, quietly working to help people without wanting or expecting praise or recognition. That was Sir Jason, in a nutshell, and now me. I will never forget hearing those famous words, "Kneel, Raymond Winters. Arise, Sir Raymond, Knight Commander, Sovereign Order of St. John of Jerusalem." I felt my father was with me when I kneeled down and we stood up together!

Our Posts and Titles within the Order
1985

My Father was appointed: Knight of Grace, Knight Grand Cross of Grace, Grand Samaritan of the Order. Later Appointments include Member of the Grand Council.

Lady Jeannette Winters, Dame of Grace, Sovereign Order of Saint John of Jerusalem

2010

I am now a Hereditary Knight Commander, Samaritan of the Order, Grand Hospitaler International, and Head of Commandery.

VOWS OF A KNIGHT

These are the vows of a Knight:

In the name of the Father and of the Son and of the Holy Spirit. Amen.

Upon the true faith of a Christian, may God witness that I hereby vow and dedicate myself as a servant of Christ and the poor, the first qualifications of a true Knight / Lady of the Sovereign Order of Saint John of Jerusalem.

As a member of this religious body, I promise to be faithful and loyal to the ideals of the Order of Saint John of Jerusalem, to do everything in my power to contribute to its glory, protection, prosperity, support and utility; to combat anything that is detrimental to its wellbeing within the limits of the laws of my country and to conduct myself always as a true knight of Christ and a person of honour.

Believing that Christ will grant me a special token of His favour, I, therefore, in all humility, charity and respect, agree to join with every sincere and godly Christian of whatever church to bring about by prayer and by deed the salvation of the Christian World by helping to promote a lasting Christian Unity as well as a lasting Unity of the Order of Saint John according to the stipulations prompted by World Seat of the Order in Malta.

I will adorn my knighthood with true charity, the mother and the solid foundation of all virtues.

I will wear on my person the famous Maltese Eight-pointed Cross, to constantly remind me of my religious vows of always bearing in my heart the Cross of Jesus Christ, adorned with the virtues that attend it. So help me God.

Signature of Postulant

N.B. This vow is subject to approval from World Seat of the Sovereign Order of Saint John of Jerusalem before coming into effect.

Chapter 11

A New Way to Live

If you can fill the unforgiving minute
With sixty seconds' worth of distance run—
Yours is the Earth and everything that's in it,
And—which is more—you'll be a Man, my son!

The poem, *IF*, by Rudyard Kipling, given to me by my father to memorize when I was twelve, and then given by me to my son when he was twelve, gave me guideposts to follow throughout my life. After my dad's passing, I realized it had even more significance. My dad believed in filling every second of his life with something. "Don't waste time. Get out there and live while you can," he said. Live every second of your life. In the last line of the poem, all the fatherly wisdom is summed up by saying, IF you do your best to follow this advice you'll get everything you want and "you'll be a Man, my son!"

It was my father's death that propelled me on a journey of self-discovery to find out who I was without him in my life. My depression after his death and my writing forced me to look into my own self and my own life and it gave me the courage to look at all of it in a real way. After your life is over, I think the most important thing is being able to look back and ask, *"Did I make a difference? Did I effect change? Did I move people in a positive way? Did I try? Did I give more than I took?"*

My father made a difference. He tried to live his life like the poem. He tried not to judge people and always saw both sides of the picture. He believed in doing the best he could and in being responsible for his own actions. He made many mistakes along the

91

way but never stopped trying to better himself. He gave away more than he got and would do it without even telling anyone. After his death, I discovered he donated money to many charities and particularly animal causes, never mentioning it to anyone! He believed it was better to do it quietly, without receiving a reward.

Right now, Sir Jason Winters Tea is sold in Japan, Korea, Australia, the Philippines, Indonesia, Canada, USA, United Kingdom, South Africa, Hong Kong, South Korea, Singapore, China, Papua New Guinea, New Zealand, Malaysia, Taiwan, Netherlands, Thailand, Cambodia, Viet Nam, and via the Internet all over the world. This all started from a man who had cancer and decided not to die. He had a wonderful life and changed many people's lives in the process, including my own.

After my father's death I took his philosophies and combined them with my own: "What if I can make a difference? What if I can help people? What if I change my attitude? What If?" My dad would often say, "you can make a difference," and "you do make a difference," and that is what is on the label of every box of tea. My dad believed in loyalty to friends. I've done my best to pass these philosophies along to my children because, for me, part of being a man is not just being a good husband and a good father. I support my children in whatever they want to try and like my father told me, I tell them, "you are special, your life has meaning, and you do make a difference in the world."

It took me years to really believe this in myself and I want my children to get it a little quicker. So I tell my daughters not to base their lives solely on making their boyfriends happy. Sometimes my daughters will come home upset because someone called them names or, said "I don't like your eyebrows," or "Your hair looks mousey." Girls can be cruel. When my kids are feeling insecure, I tell them, "Not everyone is going to like you and that's OK. Try not to ever let anyone else dictate how you feel." My daughter Ashley wants to sing and I help support her with that. My daughter

Sarah wants to work in the company one day and I support her in that goal. My son RayRay likes the theatre and wants to act on Broadway. They know they can talk to me about anything. I believe you can't just tell a child to have faith; you have to show them. I try to teach them by example. As much as I try to be a good person, we all have our struggles. I get up in the morning and think, "I'm going try to be a good person today," and then people cut me off in traffic—we all know how that goes! We are all works in progress.

Chapter 12

A Wonderful Ride

I set out to write this book because I wanted people to understand Sir Jason and his life the way I do. Few people in this world truly stand out in the crowd or have that certain something, something that makes them different or interesting or both. You can't put your finger on it. Whatever it was, I miss it. I miss him. My father was one of those people. He never took the easy way out. He always chose the road less traveled. I have finally come to a place within myself that allowed me to write about him, about his life, what he liked, how he thought and what he taught me. Here was a man who came from humble beginnings in war-torn England, who grew up poor, never even riding in a car until he was seventeen. His life experience, his philosophy, and the unique way in which he looked at life, has touched the lives of many hundreds of thousands of people, worldwide. He had faith—faith in life, himself, and in God.

I often think about what I would do if I had one more day with my dad. It would be the simple little things I would like to do. Surely, I'd go back to Sherwood Forest in England with him, and I'd go to Taco Bell. We would have whatever we wanted on the menu. I would keep his car. It was an old Saturn. He could buy any car he wanted but he was happy with the Saturn. He loved that car. Most importantly, it would be nice just to be with him and let him know that I was thankful and happy with him, and to have that one extra day.

What If?

Sir Jason always postulated:

What If I Change My Attitude?
What If I Can Make a Difference?
What If I Can Help People?
What If?

I realize that my father tried to show me a better way to live life—
I mean really live, not just go through life working 9 to 5 and
never looking up at the sky and wondering what it was all about.
But getting out there and being the best I can be—really trying—
no matter how big or how insignificant the task may be.

Thoreau wrote: "Most men lead lives of quiet desperation and
go to the grave with the song still in them." To me this means
most people die without really having lived or even trying to make
a difference.

As my father put it, "What is your song, Raymond?"

"Get up there on stage, dance, sing karaoke, put yourself out
on a limb, give that speech in front of 5 or 500 people, travel, do
your best at whatever job you have, most of all, live every second
of every day, thank God for being here, love your wife and kids
and don't ever feel sorry for me—I've lived a great life!" he said
to me many times.

Well, Dad, you did make a difference in this world, you left it
a better place than you found it. You helped many people; you
helped me. I think about you every day. Your life had and has
meaning, and yes, it has been a wonderful ride.

I want to continue my father's legacy, carry on his work so I
can help as many people as possible. His most favored poem, *IF,*

is a guidepost but its ideals are actually very hard to achieve. I believe that life is about making the effort. Sir Jason was different in the way he lived his life. It was part of his nature and part of what made him special. "It's been a wonderful ride," he would say to me.

Before he died, he realized that he really was loved, and after he died, I realized that he loved me more than I ever gave him credit for.

If I had the chance, I would do the whole thing over again, taking time to savor the parts of life that are so fleeting.

In an interview, someone once asked me what I would write on Sir Jason's tombstone if he had one. What a great question. I would use this excerpt from the poem, *Invictus* by William Ernest Henley.

It matters not how strait the gate,
How charged with punishments the scroll,
I am the master of my fate:
I am the captain of my soul.

As for me, Dad, I'm still writing my song....

Bonus Material

Letters

Letters about Sir Jason from around the world.

Lady Jeanette Winters, Dame of Grace

I can't believe it has been 54 years since I met Jason. To a 19-year-old girl, he was a knight in shining armor. I remember I short-changed him a dime and he said, "Don't worry, I will come back to get it," and he did. That's how my life with him started.

We spent nearly 30 years together; through tough times and good times we were a family unit, always taking care of each other. We had five beautiful children. We traveled a lot and saw much of the world and finally settled in Las Vegas. Even though Jason and I were no longer together, we were still friends and I felt I could still depend on him, and I did from time to time.

He will always be my knight in shining armor. I loved him when I married him, I loved him when we were divorced, and I still love him today. You never truly get over your first love.

I am so proud of my eldest son Raymond for continuing his father's work.

Las Vegas, Nevada

Yuji Ishikawa

What I learnt from Sir Jason Winters is to always have a smile and hold everyone in esteem with appreciation.

These points are stamped indelibly in my mind.

And I will never forget his impressive words I heard on his first visit to Japan.

Once I asked Sir Jason a question: "What is your dream?"

He said "The peace of the world."

His words have affected every aspect of my life.

Yuji Ishikawa

Tokyo, Japan

『ジェイソン氏から学んだことは、ジェイソンウインターズティーとともに永遠に
価値あるものとして、私の心に刻まれます。
どんなときにも笑顔を忘れないこと、他を尊重し感謝の言葉を心がける大切さは
忘れられません。
そして氏が来日した時に残された言葉は印象的でした。
夢は何ですかという問いに、「世界平和」と言った時の氏の言葉はこれからの
私の人生の羅針盤になるとおもいます。』

Sir Gary Samer, KGSJ

There have been very few people in my life, who, upon meeting them, left a deep impression within me of having just met someone special. As the Australian/New Zealand agent for Sir Jason Winters' products, I knew Sir Jason's life story and the efficacy of his outstanding herbal formulations. But everything changed when Sir Jason came Down Under for a publicity tour to help our new business. Here was a man who was larger than Life, a true visionary who was more than his life story. He was a famous personality who "walked his talk." He was so passionate about helping other people, no matter who they were or what their station in life. His knowledge, and more importantly (in my opinion) his *experience*, in helping suffering humanity regain its health, was astounding. And for every single person he ever met, his message to them was: "Your life matters. You DO make a difference."

Sir Jason and I had a close, personal relationship. When we first met we immediately recognized this connection. We were kindred spirits who could share everything that we found to be important in life, even though I was in awe of his international awards, especially his knighthood. He was a true gentleman, full of grace and compassion, yet so down to earth and fun to be with.

If anyone ever doubts their ability to make a positive contribution to life, thinking they are not important enough or famous enough, Sir Jason was a perfect example. Over the past thirty years, his books and products have had a phenomenal impact on the lives of tens of millions of people around the world. He made sure that his own life mattered: that he did make a difference and left the world a better place because of his life.

I was so honored and privileged to be nominated by Sir Jason to receive a Knighthood in the same Order as Sir Jason: The

Sovereign Order of St John, Knights of Malta, the oldest continuous order of chivalry in the world today. I was invested into the Order by 96-year-old Baron Vella Haber, the same man to invest Sir Jason decades previously. I was joined by Sir Jason's son, Sir Raymond, which increased the honor and solemnity of the occasion. The Order has served humanity continuously for over 962 years.

Now it will be up to those of us who follow to make a difference in the world. I hope and pray that I can be of service to the sick and poor to even a minor extent that the "Great White Knight of God," Sir Jason Winters, achieved in his lifetime.

Sir Gary Samer KGSJ SOSJ
Knight of Grace
Sovereign Order of St John
Knights of Malta
Coffs Harbour, Australia

Dame Commander Joyce Darmanin

Hereditary Knight Commander Sir Jason Winters:

A testimony

Have you ever tasted something so good that you though its taste would linger on forever? Well! So was it with Sir Jason Winters. You did not need to be with him for long before he won you over by his gentle disposition, his sincerity and his humility. Indeed all about him was so real. No artificiality or superficiality, no pretensions of any sort. For a moment you'd even doubt that this was really Sir Jason Winters there in front of you.

Within the Vella Haber family of Malta, Sir Jason Winters is considered to be a friend and a gentleman beyond the reach of many. We first came to know of him when my father, Baron K. Vella Haber, in his capacity of International Grand Prior of the Sovereign Order of Saint John of Jerusalem and Head of the Supreme Council, welcomed Sir Jason into the Order. Sir Jason was in fact one of number of knights worldwide who visited Malta in order to receive their official investiture here on this island back on October 13, 1985. The ceremony was held in the historical shrine of Saint Agatha on the Catacombs, which shrine belongs to the Community of the Missionary Society of Saint Paul in Rabat and it was followed by a Gala Dinner for all the participants. A truly wonderful and unforgettable occasion. Eventually, Sir Jason was promoted to all the higher ranks within the Order up to the rank of Member of the Supreme Council.

One cannot but mention that Sir Jason Winters was a dear friend of Knight Commander Dr. Bernard Jensen, also of international renown and author of several books related to health and well-being. It was not only a pleasure to know these two gentlemen but an honour indeed. They were all out to help mankind in general, each through their respective fields of study and activities. Sir Jason's tea had found its way into our kitchen way before anyone in Malta knew what green tea was. Indeed, we all remember so well, it was like talking about this strange thing, the green tea, that very few were willing to experiment with.

Some, I am sure, must even have thought that we were all a wee bit strange. Indeed this tea also had to go through tight medical checks at the customs department, such as, "What on earth is this green tea?" For us, however, it was a pleasure to open the kitchen cupboard and see Sir Jason's face giving you a warm smile at any hour in the day! Years on, green tea has found its way into all our homes as we have all become so more health conscious. Sir Jason Winters was therefore speaking about his green tea when none would even give it a thought or a fair fight. How right he was to advocate its use!

Back to Sir Jason the man. He was in constant contact with my father even though we have to remember that these were the days, even though not so long ago, when one would have to post his letter and expect no answer for it before at least two months or even three. How unrealistic and impossible it already seems! But yes! Sir Jason and Baron K. Vella Haber would write to each other about their interests and experiences. They would share information, as Baron Vella Haber has spent most of his years studying medicinal plants and their use.

On one occasion Sir Jason had even told my father that since he had become a member of the Order, his business had thrived and he was doing so very well. Now, we must believe that his business was already flourishing long before he became a Knight but perhaps, his now-heightened sense of appreciation for all he had, his increased sense of altruism compounded with his desire to help others, made him even more conscious of all that was happening in his life: his flourishing business, his willingness to be of assistance to others, his desire to make a difference in a world that was slowly becoming too individualistic and detached.

104

Sir Jason was always a wonderful man in all respects and he certainly did not need the Order to improve on that. However the Sovereign Order of Saint John of Jerusalem gave him a more noble aim to work for. The vows he took during his investiture ceremony made him more aware of the needs of all those around him.

Yes, Sir Jason was already all this before he ever became a Knight, but now he felt that he was part of this big thing called the Sovereign Order of Saint John of Jerusalem and that he would, from now on, function under its wing for the glory of one and all. His was not only a desire to help others but rather became a duty. Baron K. Vella Haber had also honored him with a decree wherewith he could operate his clinic under the auspices of the Order. This gave him a greater sense of belonging, that feel-good factor that is, after all, so fulfilling. The following is a letter to my father from the office of Sir Jason in Las Vegas, which letter is dated July 27, 1999. It bears testimony of all this and reveals so much to us all.

Dear Mqs. K. Vella Haber,

I am writing to tell you about the good news from our President, Sir Jason Winters KGSJ. Since the day he was knighted in Malta, he has spoken about your great Order on radio, television and in the print media in seventy countries of the world.

The great honour that has come to him is that Sir Jason Winters KGSJ has now received the certificate of honour from the United States Congress. He is the first knight of the Order to be honoured in such a high fashion. Although at this time he is lecturing in China and Malaysia, he wanted me to write and thank you and the Order for all that you have done for him.

His book, available in nine languages, has now become so popular it has sold twelve million copies. In the book he praises the Order of Saint John highly. The Government Grant that Sir Jason received to do more herbal research in the jungles of the world is very useful. He credits it all to you and the Order, for when he was knighted in Malta, HRH Prince Charles heard about it and started a correspondence with Sir Jason that has helped change the world.

And now the good news: Sir Jason was just appointed the President of the World Federation of Integrated Medicine, an organisation that gets the medical doctors and alternative therapies to work together for the benefit of mankind.

We, his employees worldwide, wish to thank you for honouring Sir Jason years ago, thereby giving him the opportunity to serve humanity in a more powerful way. Thousands of letters reach us each month from happy people. And so, millions of people in China, Malaysia, Singapore, the Philippines and Indonesia now know about the great Order of S.O.S.J., the Church and the wonderful work accomplished by Mqs. K. Vella Haber.

May God continue to bless you always.

Christopher Robins, Mgr.

Years later we even had the pleasure to know and later meet his son, Sir Raymond. What a wonderful person he is! If you knew Sir Jason, you could not but expect to meet another genuine and true person. For Sir Raymond is as much of a gentleman as his father was and this we consider to be as great a compliment as anyone could ever shower on him. Knight Commander Sir Raymond Winters, like his father before him, was also honoured with the office of Samaritan of the Order by Decree nr.05 of 2005 and he too promotes the Order worldwide. His last tribute to his father is the "Sir Jason Winters Award" which further bears testimony to the loyalty that the Winters family has towards the Order. As the Order of Saint John, we even featured an article about the Sir

Jason Winters Award in one of our publications, as we deemed it to be an excellent example of how one could be an ambassador at large of the Order.

We saw Knight Commander Sir Raymond Winters in 2010 when, with his beautiful consort Mia and friends from Australia and Malaysia, he visited the island of Malta to receive his official investiture as Knight Commander of the S.O.S.J. from the hands of International Grand Prior, Baron. K. Vella Haber. On this occasion he also introduced two new knights, Chev. Gary Samer and Chev. Steven Soh Teck Toh, into the Order. This ceremony was held in the 16th century palazzo, Casa Bernard, in Rabat, Malta, incidentally only a kilometer away from the chapel where his own father had been knighted 25 years before! Commander Sir Raymond frequently tells us how he would like to follow in his father's footsteps. How closer to it can you get?

Yes, it is, and will always be, a pleasure to think of Sir Jason and his son Raymond. Again I will say that you do not have to be near a person to be with him, to treasure his friendship and loyalty. One moment and you are there forever.

Dame Commander Joyce Darmanin
Rabat, Malta

Tony and Marco Urera

(written by A.M. Urera, with contribution from Marco Urera)

Feb. 12, 2011

In 1987, as I was preparing for a trip from the Philippines to New York for a business conference, my son Marco related to me how he wanted to be of help to his former classmate who was diagnosed with brain cancer. Marco and some friends had done some research on cancer, and he said that he would like me to get some cans of Jason Winters' herbal tea for his former classmate.

I was given the phone number to call, which I immediately called by long distance telephone, and I made arrangements to visit the office of Sir Jason Winters. I therefore included in my itinerary a stopover at Las Vegas, where, as arranged, I was to meet with Sir Jason, and get some tea cans for Marco's classmate. I did not know much about cancer at the time, except that this was a dreaded disease and that there was no cure for it. I was skeptical but I would do what could help a suffering classmate of my son's. It might be a wild goose chase, but it wouldn't hurt to try to help.

In October that year, I was in his office in Las Vegas. He must have sensed through my probing questions that I did not believe that JW Tea could help Marco's friend. Sir Jason related to me his bout with cancer, he showed me his book. He also let me see the doctor's account of how his cancer had disappeared after he drank the tea-from-leaves combination that has now become to be labelled as JW Tea. He had pictures of himself when he was afflicted, and now right before me was a wholesome Sir Jason Winters—healthy, tall, well-built man that he was. I was also able to read and see many letters written to thank him for the tea, and how they had been cancer-cell free after taking the JW Tea! He had in fact been knighted for his contributions in helping people to be healthy.

I came back to the Philippines with five cans of tea that Sir Jason gave me gratis! He told me that he would be coming to Manila for a radio interview in early 1988, and he would like to also meet Marco and his classmate.

Unfortunately, Marco's friend died in December. He was only able to take very little of the tea because his mouth could not even open for eating. His jaw somehow locked due to his ailment.

We forgot about Sir Jason, until he called me in Manila, in 1988. He was here for a radio interview at DZMM, I believe it was. I accompanied him to the station, where he was interviewed for about five minutes. The interview became so popular, he was then taken to a TV booth in the same building where the radio station was, where his interview was continued. As I sat in the studio, watching his interview, I could hear telephone calls from people who wanted to ask questions and to ask where and how they could get his tea. Somehow he gave our office phone number, where he said he would be sending the tea for those who wanted it. For what I thought was going to be a three-minute interview on TV, he was actually interviewed for about 15 minutes, maybe even more, with plenty of people wanting to ask many more questions.

After the radio and TV interviews, he was also interviewed by newspaper reporters. All these resulted in hundreds of phone calls to our office by people who learned about him in the different interviews. Our phones at the office had never been so busy!

When Marco and I had a meeting with him after all the busyness of his activities, we told him we were not interested in distributing the tea in Manila. We advised him to find distributors, since our interest was only for Marco's friend, who had already passed away. But he told us that he would leave some tea with us to give to people who heard him talk. He said that just because one person died before he could have the tea did not mean we should not help others who need it.

At this point he convinced us that being in business with the tea was secondary only to being of help to others. Where would they get the tea after they had heard his talk on radio and TV, he asked us.

This was how we got started in distributing Jason Winters' Tea. We started by giving away some tea at the beginning. Then Sir Jason sent us more tea, which we began to sell. We did not have to advertise, people just came buying it! And for about 15 years, people got hold of his books and testimonials and they came to our office for his tea. Many, many people just came with stories and testimonies they volunteered about how the tea strengthened the immune system of sick people who got well, some with cancer, some with other diseases. Many also came to volunteer to distribute the tea; they came to buy the tea, sold it, and came back again for some more!

Sir Jason Winters' tea and other products he formulated became known in the Philippines for their value—the value from a man who dedicated himself to traveling around the world looking for local ingredients and natural products that helped one way or another in supporting people's efforts to get well.

Having seen how Sir Jason Winters' products have helped people, we will continue to have his products available through our office when and if they look for those products. People just continue to know about him through his many publications, and we will be pleased to serve them, as we have been doing in the past 23 years!

Manila, Philippines

Mr. Handy Wang

Sometimes in life we find someone, who through the course of dramatic circumstances, is able to produce something worthwhile for the good of mankind.

I was fortunate enough to have known and worked with Sir Jason Winters, who, through his struggle to help fight his cancer after he experienced a death sentence, accidentally discovered the tea formula restoring health to him. Now, along with his son Sir Raymond Winters, we continue to help people.

Indeed, we cannot help everyone, but we feel very happy because we can make Sir Jason's story available more broadly to the public.

Now, I would like to continue to provide the best for those in need of help and continue the mission that has been put in place by Sir Jason Winters.

Handy Wang
Jakarta, Indonesia

Sir Steven Soh, KGSJ SOSJ

"Come, come and drink this tea and feel better," my friend Justin Goh called out across his office as I entered it. As I drank the tea, he showed me the can. I liked the taste and sometime after that a friend gave me a can and told me that I would know the efficacy of the tea if I drank a strong cup or two before I went to bed and that the next morning, I would know its value. Sure enough, the next morning, when I woke up, I was convinced there and then and began to drink the tea regularly.

It was around 1990 that the agent for this part of the world asked me if I wanted to be the sole agent for Malaysia. As I already had a multi-level direct sales company, I accepted the agency.

It was a success from the first minute. The sales kept on climbing and climbing. At the time that Sir Jason Winters came for a visit here to do a road show, the agent put Sir Jason up in an apartment.

When I met Sir Jason the first time, we took a liking for each other straightaway. He struck me as a very down-to-earth man and that we blended with people very well. I remembered when he gave a talk in Segamat, Malaysia, telling his life story. He cried and so did the whole audience. His story touched the hearts of all present there.

We seemed to understand each other very well and felt if we could do something good for each other, we would do it willingly and heartily before he passed away. He told his son Sir Raymond to recommend me for the knighthood that I received in February last year.

I felt a great loss, losing a very good friend and benefactor. In time, all of us will meet again and I am looking forward to that meeting.

Sir Steven Soh, KGSJ SOSJ
Knight of Grace
Sovereign Order of St John
Knights of Malta
Malaysia

Mr. Eric Wong

I know about Sir Jason Winters through the introduction of my respectful friend, Mr. TH Leung. Mr. Leung was a patient who suffered from a final stage of snuff cancer in the mid 1980s and had tried to follow whatever doctors asked him to do, including cobalt radiation and all sorts of orthodox methods and treatments. After being disappointed with most of the traditional treatments, he finally decided to reach out to the world, finding whatever he could to improve his health situation. Lastly he found Jason Winters Tea. After having it for years, he miraculously recovered from his sickness. It has now been over 20 years since his recovery and he is now joining with us to share his experience with other people.

It is a gift to know Sir Jason Winters and learn about his stories. Sir Jason Winters visited us in Hong Kong in April 2000. We were all excited to meet him. It is our honor to work with him and being one of the distribution agents for these products that were formulated by him. Selling Jason Winters products is not only a business to us but also a mission for us to help others.

Of course when people get sick, it is important to seek medical advice from a doctor immediately. I cannot say there is any miracle to using the herbs, but from real life examples, it is definitely my pleasure when people give merits for the use of these herbs and introduce these meritorious herbs to their friends in need. There is nothing more vital than health. No matter how many millions you are worth, it means nothing when you cannot enjoy good health. After all, health belongs to your own self. Always treasure health and enjoy life.

Eric Wong
Health Watchers Limited
Hong Kong SAR

Excerpt from
The Sir Jason Winters Story

In the exact words of my father as he wrote them over 30 years ago, from his book originally titled *Killing Cancer*, now known as *The Sir Jason Winters Story*. This book is in print in 17 languages and various dialects of the Chinese language, with millions of copies in print since 1980.

TERMINAL CANCER

I walked into the Cobalt Radiation Department for the first time and was filled with despair. This department took care of patients suffering from head and neck cancer. There were about 20 patients in the waiting room, and I took my place among them. My heart was thumping, and with good reason, for the faces all around me showed fear and depression. I could smell death in the air. Most of the people had hardly any hair left, due to the chemotherapy treatment. Ashtrays were scattered around the room and nearly everyone was smoking heavily. When I mentioned that smoking is bad for health, one patient said, "Well, it's too late for us now anyway, isn't it?"

One by one patients had their names called and they would disappear behind a large lead door. When they came out they looked worse than before—and left hurriedly. I was worried, as I had no idea what was behind that door. Would I, too, soon have no hair and that look of terror in my eyes? I heard the nurse call my name, and as if in a daze, found myself following her into the treatment room.

I had first noticed the swelling on the side of my neck when taking a steam bath at the YMCA. Although 46 years old, I was in top physical condition, running and swimming each day. I had a great wife, five kids and a good income. I smoked thirty cigarettes a day and did some real hard drinking at least once a week. Rye whisky was my favorite.

The lump seemed to ache deep inside my throat. I was worried. I bought some lozenges and tried to forget about it. As the days went by the lump got bigger and bigger, but I avoided my doctor like the plague. I was unconsciously scared of what the lump might be. After a few more weeks even my friends noticed the swelling and remarked on it. I realized that I could not avoid

116

the issue indefinitely, so I made an appointment with our family doctor.

He at once sent me to a surgeon. It resulted in dozens of X-rays, examinations at the Nuclear Medicine Center, scans, pills—and fear. At last it was decided that I must go into the hospital to have a small biopsy operation. The surgeon said it would take only half an hour and result in a scar a couple of inches long.

Soon after I checked into the hospital, a dear old lady came around with lots of strong black coffee, white sugar and cream cake. She was trying hard to serve humanity and no one ever told her she was serving what I later found out to be the very worst things a cancer patient, or anyone else for that matter, can eat and drink.

I was scared to death, especially when they placed the mask over my face and I felt myself drifting away in a wave of terror.

Suddenly, everything was black, like the darkest night. I could see nothing, but for the first time in months I realized that I was not afraid; the air was cool and I breathed deeply and with every breath I felt stronger. Soon I saw a dim light far away so I started to drift towards it. I was walking but could not feel my legs or feet. It was effortless.

Soon I realized that I was in some kind of tunnel. Once I reached the entrance I noticed that I was wearing a long brown robe and pointed slippers that were covered in white dust.

Leaving the tunnel, I was shocked by the sky. Words cannot explain how brilliantly blue it was. The pathway I had to walk was along the very peak of a line of mountains. The pathway was only six inches wide. There was a sheer drop on either side of the path, a drop that looked hundreds of feet deep. However, I could not see the bottom because there were dark clouds covering the ground far below me. From the depths of these clouds came the worst screams and moans that I had ever heard. Moans of total and complete despair. Moans I will never forget.

I had to walk carefully, or I would fall into the clouds below, and those terrible noises.

Suddenly the most brilliant of lights, so bright I could not look at it, was rushing down the path towards me. I could not move to either side to avoid it, so I crouched down and put up my arms for protection. The light passed right through me, and then I heard the nurse shouting, "More anesthetic quickly! He is regaining consciousness."

_____

When I awoke from the operation, I found that it had taken six and a half hours, and left a scar nine inches long. I saw immediately that my wife had been crying. I guess that was when I first knew for sure my condition was serious. The doctor walked in and said, "Terminal cancer. Infiltrating squamous cell carcinoma." The tumor was wrapped around my carotid artery and, to make matters even worse, was attached to the wall of my jugular vein.

After telling me three times that my condition was terminal, the doctor left me to my misery. My wife Jan went home to break the news to our five children. Thoughts of death crowded in on me from all sides. Reading, television, and radio were all drowned out by the thoughts that soon I would be gone.

The next morning, when my doctor made his rounds, he did not find me in bed. Another patient and I were having a hilarious pillow fight from our wheelchairs. The doctor was furious. "Don't you know you have terminal cancer? Don't you realize you should be in bed?" Because I was sure that all doctors are gods, I obeyed him quickly. It was not long before I was out of bed again—this time to trudge around the hospital.

I walked around the whole place five times for exercise, and when I returned it was the head nurse's turn to be furious. She said the doctor had been complaining to her about me, and once again assured me that I had terminal cancer, and must at least stay in my room.

It seemed to me that everyone was worried in case I forgot to die. The doctor even went so far as to lecture my wife on my behavior. "Doesn't he know he's got terminal cancer? Doesn't he believe me?" Many tests followed and finally it was agreed what my treatment should be. I would have five weeks of cobalt radiation on my neck and head, and then if the swelling were down, I could have radical neck surgery. That meant the removal of my tongue, jawbone, neck muscles, and also the inside of my throat. To begin with I would receive three cobalt treatments each day for five weeks.

I felt better as soon as I left the hospital and walked down the street. I felt free, even though I got a lot of stares from people gaping at the bandages around my face and neck. At least they couldn't see the tumor.

My first appointment with the cancer clinic bothered me. I had to be fitted for a plastic mask. This went right over my head like the Count of Monte Cristo mask. There were three holes in one side for it to be attached to the cobalt machine, so that I could not move my head while being bombarded with radiation. I had to go back in one week for another fitting, and this really depressed me. It got so bad that I would not let my wife tell anyone that I had cancer. I could not stand the look of fear in their faces and the way even old friends changed towards me. I would not even let my children say the word *cancer*.

The nurse in the cobalt room called my name—and it started.

For five weeks I was to see my fellow patients gradually get weaker and weaker—then I would see them no more. One friend was a big strong man and had a tumor on the side of his head. After many cobalt treatments his right eye started running, so they sewed it closed. I will always remember the terror in his one good eye, as he looked at me in desperation. I said, "Don't worry, we will both get better," not believing it myself, of course.

My friend beamed and he shouted to all the other patients. "Did you hear that? Jason says we are both going to get better!" It was many months later that I understood what he meant and why he was so happy. Since he had discovered he had cancer, he had been told repeatedly, "Terminal, terminal." I was the first one in the whole wide world to tell him he would get better, or to offer even any hope at all. He died two days later. I started taking Valium tablets each day so that I would not break down and cry, as well as pain pills and sleeping pills.

The cobalt treatment took away my taste, made it impossible for me to make saliva, burned the right side of my face and made my hair fall out. Life was hell.

I went from 263 pounds down to 170 pounds. My knees were shaky and I could not stay awake for longer than four hours at a time. It was then that I discovered the value of pure honey and vitamin E. As I would sit on the couch in shock, after the cobalt treatment, I would eat spoonfuls of honey which I could not taste but I knew was good for me. I stopped losing weight. I smeared the vitamin E on my burned face, and soon there was a great improvement. Doctors at the cancer clinic remarked how well I was taking the treatment. I told them what I was doing and they said that this was fine, but I was not to mention it to the others.

That remark puzzled me no end. I thought about it constantly. I did tell the others about it and they all started the same treatment with good results. But the doctors did not want me to tell anyone about it. The only answer I could figure out to this scared the heck out of me, but it probably saved my life. I started to realize that doctors are not gods after all. Maybe they can make mistakes too.

If that was right, then maybe they had made a mistake about me. They all kept telling me to get my affairs in order, and prepare to die, but perhaps I didn't have to die.

The next day the surgeon called me into his office. He had decided to operate on me as soon as possible. Radical neck surgery. Removal of tongue, jaw bone and neck muscles. He went into great detail about the operation. When I asked him if I would live any longer from having the surgery, he said probably not. I looked him straight in the eye and said, "No."

The doctor said, "What do you mean, no?"

I said, "No operation." Then I stood up and walked out of his office. My heart was singing. I was going to keep my tongue and die in one piece.

Many times the doctor called my wife to tell her to get me into the hospital. Everyone was trying to get me there, even though they knew that I would die anyway. I couldn't understand it. I wondered who these people thought they were, asking me to have this terrible operation.

HEALING HERBS

Once I started learning about herbs as medicine, I became excited, especially after my letdown with laetrile. The most powerful ancient herb for tumors seemed to come from Asia. I went to every herbalist in my area, then telephoned others across the country. They had never heard of it except in old books from Asia. The more difficult this herb became for me to find the more determined I was to have it. *Buddha called it herbalene.*

When I learned that it was available in Singapore, I started thinking about traveling there. The only problem was money. We had six thousand dollars to our name, did not own a house or anything else worthwhile that I could get a loan on. Also we had five kids to support. But still, we all felt that this was a matter of life and death. I had many credit cards left over from my more affluent days and I figured I would use these to pay travel expenses. If I survived, then I would pay them back, and if not, my wife would have to declare bankruptcy. So it came about that with our two youngest children, my wife and I boarded a plane—destination Singapore. The fact that my two children had to support me, one under each arm, caused the Singapore immigration some concern. For a moment it was touch and go on whether they would let me into the country. We explained that I was merely airsick, which I am sure they did not believe, as the tumor was obvious to all. They decided in our favor and we soon found ourselves at the hotel. I lost no time in looking for the herb, which was not available in the stores in Singapore. At last I came upon an old lady living a distance from town, who cultivated the herb.

Evidently she dug up the roots and boiled fifty pounds in a large container. After boiling it vigorously for twenty-six hours, she was left with a liquid concentrate, which she sold for a very

122

high price. Usually sold in half-ounce bottles, she was surprised when I asked for one pint. I was told it would definitely get rid of my cancer. I can remember that I held that bottle with great reverence—after all, this was the very thing that the great Buddha suggested for tumors. I could hardly wait to get back to the hotel to start drinking it. The directions were to take one-eighth of a teaspoonful in a large glass of water, once each day, until well.

For ten days I took the medicine, and when nothing happened I doubled the dose. The tumor, although not getting any bigger stayed the same size exactly. A hurried visit to the old lady brought merely a shrug. She had no idea why it had not worked. She said, "Well, at least it's stopped growing," and that was it. My wife insisted that we buy another pint from her, even though we still had a lot left over. Jan was so impressed by the old lady's knowledge that she figured even if it did not cure cancer, it would prevent her getting it. Both her parents had died of the disease.

We left Singapore feeling very low indeed. I felt the herb did not work, and maybe that was why it didn't. We left for our next destination, which was Tucson, Arizona.

Years before, I had been a stunt man and a bit actor in Hollywood. We had made a few films with Audie Murphy in a place called Old Tucson, just a few miles from Tucson. Old Tucson was built in the Old West style for Hollywood. Many western movies were made there, including *Apache Agent*, in which I played. I had learned at that time about a tea which most Indians, especially Mexican Indians, drank for health, and that's what prompted our visit. In Arizona we soon located the herb, known as chaparral, or the creosote bush (*Larrea divaricata*). Once again we heard that this remedy had been passed down through the ages and may prevent or get rid of cancer.

We stayed at the Santa Rita Hotel in Tucson, then moved to a small motel with a kitchen. The chaparral tea which I had to make five times each day was putrid, and smelled as bad as it tasted. It was enough to make a healthy man sick, but I persisted. It seemed to do nothing at all, except make me sick, but looking back now I feel that although I was not getting better, I was not getting worse. But at the time, so obsessed with death and dying, I was too depressed to notice.

In Tucson, a nutritionist who learned of my condition told us that in Europe there were many old remedies for different ills, even cancer. He said that because there is socialized medicine there (free doctors and hospitals), doctors don't expect to become rich overnight. Because of this they are more open to inexpensive alternative therapies. He said that if ever he became ill, he would return to England for that reason alone. And so, as a last resort, we decided to visit England.

With five pounds of chaparral and a pint and a half of the Singapore potion, we boarded the plane for London. We had already spent most of our cash and were now on credit cards. That was the only time in my life that I have ever appreciated credit. In one clinic I met HRH Prince Charles, who gave me hope.

Now I have dozens of relatives in England, but I would not let my wife contact any of them. I did not want them to see me like this, and I wanted no tears. This is the part of the trip that I enjoyed, because this was the country I was born in, and it did me good to see the beautiful countryside once more. In my heart I knew that the visit was not really necessary, but just returning home meant defeat, and going to England postponed the inevitable for a while.

The Archbishop of Canterbury introduced me to red clover (*Trifolium pratense*), the Gypsy health drink that is supposed to be good for many things. Evidently there is a big difference between red and white clover blossoms, with the white being inferior. White clover is sold all over North America as being the best.

Chopped up clover blossoms make a very nice tea, which I started drinking, also at the rate of five glasses each day. This meant that I was busy making tea all day, first with the Asian herb, then chaparral, then red clover.

On the fourth day I became very ill indeed. My legs were shaking and I felt terribly sick. I had to stay in bed. I stopped taking all the herbs and readied myself for death. Our credit cards were promptly confiscated and we found we owed many thousands of dollars. Bill collectors were calling on the telephone and knocking on the door constantly; we were all very worried. My youngest son, Robin, was sent home from school because he broke down and started crying. When asked why, he said, "My dad is dying of cancer."

As a last resort, I started back on the herbal teas again. One morning, I can remember it well, I was at my lowest ebb. I thought to heck with it, I'll mix all the herbs together.

THE MIXTURE

It was five minutes to ten on a Wednesday morning. I made the tea combination and a miracle happened.

I could feel it with that first swallow. It seemed to ring a distant bell, a long-past memory. It screamed at me that this was what I needed. Strength seemed to pour through my body. That day I made a gallon of the tea and drank it all. When my family walked through the door they could see the difference in my face. I was enthusiastic, excited and overjoyed. Tears filled all of our eyes. We did not understand what had happened but we all knew that something wonderful had taken place. Day after day I drank one gallon regularly. Strength and vitality returned, but mostly it was my frame of mind. I was going to live, I knew it. All depression left me, all morbid thoughts. The more excited I became the smaller the tumor got; the smaller the tumor became, the more I got excited. Within three weeks the tumor had gone completely. Everyone called it a miracle, because in nine weeks I returned to work. I was not as healthy as before, I was healthier, and God, how I enjoyed every minute of life.

My case became well known throughout the news media and people with terminal cancer started lining up outside the door, just to talk to me. They all wanted the tea. Then my local priest called me into his office and said, "Look, Jason, I know, and so do you, that you have found something for good health. Why, my hemorrhoids, which I have suffered with for twenty years, disappeared in two weeks of drinking your tea. Many other things are happening to people drinking it, too. Good things. You have something here, and if you do nothing about it you will be guilty of the sin of omission. But if you do decide to do something about it, you can expect to be persecuted severely. The officials won't let you ruin a multimillion-dollar-a-year business without a fight, and they have the money and the power to ridicule you, and to threaten you."

After much thought, I decided to tell my story to the world. A small newspaper took up the story first, which resulted in over three hundred telephone calls and a thousand letters, plus a big lineup outside the door, from 8 AM until past midnight. Everyone wanted the tea. Separately, the herbs would not work for me; together they were a miracle. I started importing the ingredients and mixing them in five-ounce bags, which I would give to anyone who wanted some. In exchange they would give a donation so that I could get more herbs. Thank God for Dr. Ian Pearce, M.D., for explaining why the formula works.

The radio station told my story, which increased the customers tenfold. Never in the history of the radio station had they received so many calls as they did about that particular program.

One man with a brain tumor received such help that the doctors pronounced him well. Without my permission he had advertising made up about my tea. He wanted the world to know about it—he wanted to help everyone. He got me into trouble and my first persecutions began.

People started flying in to see me from Australia, Germany, and many other places in the world, and I was flooded under. The police became regular visitors to my place, making sure that I did not tell anyone that the herbs were any good for anything. But I didn't need to say anything. The world was so desperate for something natural that would work that I was constantly running out of herbs.

I started receiving many offers from people and companies, one even from a priest. I had never met this man before, but he came up to me and said, "Take me in as your partner and we will make a million. We can charge fifty dollars a four-ounce bag, and

I can get the hell out of this church." All this, in front of a witness! I found it hard to believe, and told him a definite "No."

Now the priest had in his congregation a particularly violent man who needed help desperately. The priest, mad at me for not accepting his offer, set this man on me. He actually attacked me once in the church. The priest would incite the man, whom I will call Mr. H. Strangely enough, one of the first letters reporting benefits from the tea came from Mr. H.'s wife. So furious were the priest and Mr. H. that they typed letters to magazines and newspapers, and sometimes even to dying people, saying, "Mr. Winters never had cancer, and if you want more information call Reverend...," and of course the letters were unsigned. So persecution and hatred came from various places. When a national magazine ran a 28-page story on my experiences and the tea, they took three months to put it together, and interviewed hundreds of people involved.

As far as the editors are concerned the tea works, and now they are steady drinkers of it themselves. At the time the article was being prepared, the Canadian version of the FDA showed up and went through our files, taking the names of all our customers and confiscating all the tea we had. By this time I had three thousand people relying on me for the tea. They took up a collection and I left for Nassau in the Bahamas, where I set up a company.

When the article came out in the magazine, we started receiving over 2000 orders each day, and that has continued with absolutely no advertising whatsoever. We had to hire all the unemployed people we could get to help us, and still the business grew. Over one thousand letters each month poured in telling of the relief obtained from all kinds of ills. Hollywood stars, politicians, all types of medical men, attorneys, truck drivers, order regularly.

Greed caused people to do some pretty terrible things—the priest previously mentioned, for instance. Knowing that I had left the country, he gathered a group of people around him and they are now selling an herbal mix using my name, knowing that it is nowhere near the same tea. A health food distribution company in Toronto also could see the money in this, and is putting out a phony tea under my name. These people are of course trading lives for dollars, and I mention this so that the reader knows enough to be careful.

I have recently turned over the formula and all rights to a large manufacturer of herbal preparations. The hatred, bitterness, greed and harassment proved too much for me to handle. Besides this, my values have changed. Money is not as important to me as being alive. I feel wonderful about life, and about God, who cured me. Greed and bitterness cause stress, and I think that stress causes cancer, so I will leave all those feelings behind.

GOOD NEWS FROM SAUDI ARABIA AND ENGLAND

People all over the world started drinking our tea, which has now become known as possibly the best health drink in the world. The only complaint we received, however was from people asking if the taste could be made a little less bitter.

It was in England where Dr. Ian Pierce, M.D., told me that one other herb was exchangeable for chaparral (the bitter one), and that was sage.

In the year 1620, a famous Arab physician claimed, "How can a man become ill, with this herb growing in the garden?" But I was to find out that there are over one hundred types of sage, some with health benefits and many without. I decided to find out for myself which herbal sage the Arabian doctor had been referring to. It was not as difficult a search as I had thought. Herbalists in the Middle East had used the same herb for centuries to treat people for every illness under the sun.

129

When I obtained some, mixed it with red clover and spice (I did this on my table in the kitchen) I was so pleased with the results that the same day I invited everyone that came to the house, including the mailman, the next-door neighbors and the local policeman, to try it. They all thought it was delicious. Yet it still got the same results as the previous blend.

Here at last we had a good drink that tasted great. But still some diehards demanded the chaparral formula. And so, for many years we produced both. There really is no need to put up with a bitter taste any more and as an alternative to coffee, regular tea and soft drinks, this is the answer. The Japanese were the first ones to put this new Jason Winters Herbal Tea into soft drink cans, and people of all ages love it.

So, if you are worried about chaparral, don't be. It seems that God helps us every step of the way.

WHY THE HERB COMBINATION WORKS

God placed a certain herb on each continent to cure illness by simply purifying the blood. Life is in the blood, and if anything purifies the blood then a person's God-given natural immunity will have a chance to take over and fight all disease.

It is as simple as that.

The herb God put in Asia will not grow elsewhere, and the same goes for chaparral of North America and red clover of Europe. If you try to grow these herbs elsewhere they do not thrive because of soil deficiencies.

Jesus spoke of one herb for purifying the blood, Buddha of another herb in Asia, and the North American spirit fathers of yet another. Now in those days, before coffee, white sugar, processed foods and fast food outlets, any one of these herbs would have done the trick on its own. However, we alive today have such toxic bodies that we don't know what good health really is; after all we have nothing to judge it by. We are fed on canned milk from birth, then doctored up cow's milk, canned baby food, graduating to hamburgers, french fries, coffee and poisonous white sugar. That is why just one of these herbs would not work on me. I was so full of toxins, as are you, that it took the combined effort of three of the most powerful herbs to bring me back to health.

I did not know it at the time, but while I was drinking the tea, at first I became sick to my stomach. I should have noticed this as a good sign. All that was happening was that the herbs were clearing my body of poison, and it was taking place so fast that it was overpowering my liver. What a person should do in that case is take it easy for three days, then start on the herbs again. Eventually the body will be pure and you will not feel sick any more.

131

On a recent trip to England I was met with open arms by the medical profession. They were eager to try my tea. One radionics practitioner tested the tea with his machine and found that it raised his energy level from 47 to 88. This may not mean much to the average reader, but to anyone in the know about radionics it is quite astounding. We immediately got calls from reporters wanting interviews and these people were not the slightest bit hesitant about printing the facts about the tea. What a difference from America where the newspapers keep well away from anything like this, unless they are accusing you of something! Even the British royal family has their own herbalist, a Mrs. Blackie, who has treated the Queen and her family for years.

The highlight of my trip to England was meeting two wonderful men, Dr. Ian Pearce and Malcolm Rae. In Dr. Pearce we found a medical doctor with an open mind. I shall always remember sitting in his cottage in Norfolk, listening to him talk about herbs. Mr. Rae, on the other hand, was one of the world's leading radionics practitioners. Sadly, he died at the end of 1979. He placed the tea on a machine and startled us by saying that the tea worked not only on the physical level, but also on the mental and spiritual planes. Why this startled me was that the old lady in Singapore had said, "This herb will bring the spiritual and mental bodies back into line with the physical body." At the time I did not understand it, but I did when Malcolm Rae explained it. It is simply a matter of treating the whole person, not just a particular illness. You must treat the mental, spiritual and physical before you can obtain perfect health.

Malcolm Rae then examined me by machine and found that although I had no cancer, I was suffering from cobalt radiation poisoning of the jawbone, but that the tea was ridding me of that slowly.

Upon our arrival back in Nassau we found thousands of complaints from people who had not received their tea, ordered weeks before. We checked back and found that all had been sent via the Post Office within two days of receiving the order. It seemed as though the powers that be had finally found a way to stop us from helping people. During a period of three months over 10,000 packets of tea disappeared in the post, and we have never found them. The customers, knowing nothing of our problems, started to write some pretty awful letters to us, some even blaming us for their spouse's death.

This of course bothered me to no end, so we kept sending out second orders free, by the thousands. In spite of all our troubles, the letters kept coming in telling of health improvements in arthritis, varicose veins, hemorrhoids, skin problems and much more. Now that the herbs are supplied by one company, these problems have been solved.

Along with complaints come pitiful, sad stories—some that have made us weep. One lady sent back the tea, saying, "My doctor says I have only a month or so to live and he doesn't want me using this stuff." And another, "My husband sneaks your tea into the hospital every night in a thermos. The doctor would be furious if he knew what it was but we told him it's brandy. He feels better each day and the doctor thinks it's his doing."

But the saddest case of all is the following. A woman of 35 came to me because she had cancer of the breast. I spoke to her about my case and she became a different person, excited and happy. She visited her doctor that afternoon and he told her that the cancer had spread to her right eye and brain. She asked, "What can I do, Doctor, shall I take herbs, laetrile, shall I pray?" His answer was "Don't waste your time on all of that stuff, it's all garbage. Just face it and get your affairs in order." The lady went home and killed herself that same day.

Please listen to me when I say that cancer does not mean death. We usually start dying as soon as we hear that word. We have been brainwashed into thinking it's a killing disease and we are supposed to die from it. The doctor may well insist that you believe him when he tells you how much time you have left. No one knows how long you have got—it's largely up to you. If you believe the doctor then you will die right on time. We have seen this on many occasions. Your life is up to you, so don't believe any doctor who condemns you to die just because he doesn't understand your illness. There are thousands of people I have met who were expected to die of cancer years ago. They all had one thing in common, and that is they agreed God is smarter than their doctor.

All I am asking you to do is to change your mind about things, and live. God gave you life, and it's up to you to keep it. Eat properly, think properly, and you will soon notice a difference.

A recent experiment in Europe was very interesting. People with cancer were gathered together, and were all asked this question: "What do you think your cancer looks like, and what do you think of the medicine that you are given to fight it?"

Group A were in accord that their cancer was like a big black rat, very strong and devouring everything, even the medicine.

Group B said that their cancer was a small lump surrounded by white cells (natural immunity) that were gradually eating the cancer away.

Although these people had the same cancer in the same degree, most of group A died and group B lived. Please think about this. Jesus said that faith can move mountains.

Dr. Fernie has another theory on cancer. He claims that cancer patients all fall into a certain category. He explained it to me this way. A woman of 45 has a husband who now devotes all his time to his business. Her children have left home either to get married or to live elsewhere. She develops breast cancer. Suddenly she is at the top of her husband's list so far as attention goes, and the children come rushing home. Could we get cancer just to get our own way? I know that if we concentrate we can eliminate pain, or make ourselves happy or sad. If Dr. Fernie is right and we unconsciously make ourselves ill, then we can just as easily make ourselves well. Faith can move mountains.

At another clinic, only a cancer patient who has passed a test as a positive thinker will be accepted. Also, the only visitors allowed in to see the patients are positive thinkers—ones who will spread hope and life and enthusiasm. It seems to work, too.

A clinic in England treats its cancer patients with a steady diet of asparagus tips. This seems to work. Yet another gets good results with massive doses of vitamins A and C, plus six glasses of carrot juice each day.

Another believes that we get cancer because our pancreas is not putting out enough enzymes to eat up the protein in our diet, so they prescribe thirty pancreatic enzymes each day.

One doctor of nutrition has had success fighting cancer with a solution made from poison ivy. One man cured cancer, he assures me, with two teaspoons of gasoline each day!

Another man with lung cancer refused to go into the hospital for the treadmill of death. He said he would not accept the fact that he had cancer, and it went away. Many say that my tea brings such hope to people who have had all hope taken away that they believe they will get well as quickly as I—so they do. Faith can move mountains. As soon as we find out that the medical profession isn't all the answer, and people are living in spite of phony death sentences, then we have to choose among many therapies.

It seems that everyone who has beaten cancer writes a book about it, and claims to know the secret and the true answer. I am not one of these. I say that seeing that it's your life you are going to save, then take the best from all of them. None of the things they recommend will hurt you, but leave out the gasoline, please; there is an oil shortage.

Let's look at it this way. If there are many types of cancers then there could be many types of natural treatments. You must of course purify your blood first. We are about to take advantage of all the knowledge gained by people who fought for their lives and won. Please remember that most of them were in worse shape than you to begin with.

First thing, when that nice little old lady shows up with the coffee, tell her to disappear and take the coffee with her. Don't let her forget the white sugar and cream because you won't be needing those either. Now, if you are in a hospital it may be a little tough because everyone knows it is almost impossible to get well in a hospital. Just be careful of what you eat. Try to get lots of fresh fruit and vegetables, raw if possible. Whole wheat bread only. Eat twenty raw almonds each day. Take five pancreatic enzymes before each meal. Don't eat canned foods, and stay away from salt. Eat twelve ounces of asparagus each day and, if it must be canned, use the Jolly Green Giant kind because it has less acid in it. Try to get lots of fresh carrot juice and drink it within an hour of being made.

One more thing. If you are going to keep on smoking, then forget about all of the above. Out of the thousands of terminal patients that I have spoken to during the last three years not one smoker has survived, and it didn't matter what he tried. Once a heavy smoker myself, I can hardly stand to be in the same room with someone who is smoking.

You must quit smoking if you want to live, and if you want to live, then you will. Faith can move mountains.

Poems

Of all the poems Dad and I read, these are my favorites. I've read them many times and they mean more to me now, I suppose, because I'm older.

Invictus

Out of the night that covers me,
Black as the Pit from pole to pole,
I thank whatever gods may be
For my unconquerable soul.

In the fell clutch of circumstance
I have not winced nor cried aloud.
Under the bludgeonings of chance
My head is bloody, but unbowed.

Beyond this place of wrath and tears
Looms but the Horror of the shade,
And yet the menace of the years
Finds, and shall find, me unafraid.

It matters not how strait the gate,
How charged with punishments the scroll.
I am the master of my fate:
I am captain of my soul.

William Ernest Henley
(1849–1903)

The things for to attain

The things for to attain;
The happy life be these, I find:
The riches left, not got with pain;
The fruitful ground, the quiet mind;
The equal friend; no grudge nor strife;
No charge of rule nor governance;

The night discharged of all care
Where wine may bear no sovereignty;
The chaste wife wise, without debate;
Such sleeps as may beguile the night;
Contented with thine own estate;
Neither wish death, nor fear his might.

Martial Valerius, Roman poet, *Epigrams X, 47*

(circa AD 40–103)

Translation by Henry Howard, Duke of Surrey

O Me! O Life!

O me! O life!... of the questions of these recurring;
Of the endless trains of the faithless—of cities fill'd with
the foolish;
Of myself forever reproaching myself, (for who more
foolish than I, and who more faithless?)
Of eyes that vainly crave the light—of the objects mean—
of the struggle ever renew'd;
Of the poor results of all—of the plodding and sordid
crowds I see around me;
Of the empty and useless years of the rest—with the rest
me intertwined; The question,
O me! so sad, recurring—What good amid these, O me, O
life?

Answer.

That you are here—that life exists, and identity;
That the powerful play goes on, and you will contribute a
verse.

Walt Whitman

142

O Captain! my Captain!

O Captain! my Captain! our fearful trip is done;
The ship has weather'd every rack, the prize we sought is won;
The port is near, the bells I hear, the people all exulting,
While follow eyes the steady keel, the vessel grim and daring:
But O heart! heart! heart!
O the bleeding drops of red,
Where on the deck my Captain lies,
Fallen cold and dead.

O Captain! my Captain! rise up and hear the bells;
Rise up—for you the flag is flung—for you the bugle trills;
For you bouquets and ribbon'd wreaths— for you the shores a-
  crowding;
For you they call, the swaying mass, their eager faces turning;
Here Captain! dear father!
This arm beneath your head;
It is some dream that on the deck,
You've fallen cold and dead.

My Captain does not answer, his lips are pale and still;
My father does not feel my arm, he has no pulse nor will;
The ship is anchor'd safe and sound, its voyage closed and done;
From fearful trip, the victor ship, comes in with object won;
Exult, O shores, and ring, O bells!
But I, with mournful tread,
Walk the deck my Captain lies,
Fallen cold and dead.

Walt Whitman

(May 31, 1819–March 26, 1892)

IF

If you can keep your head when all about you
Are losing theirs and blaming it on you;
If you can trust yourself when all men doubt you,
But make allowance for their doubting too;
If you can wait and not be tired by waiting,
Or being lied about, don't deal in lies,
Or being hated, don't give way to hating,
And yet don't look too good, nor talk too wise:

If you can dream—and not make dreams your master;
If you can think—and not make thoughts your aim;
If you can meet with Triumph and Disaster
And treat those two imposters just the same;
If you can bear to hear the truth you've spoken
Twisted by knaves to make a trap for fools,
Or watch the things you gave your life to, broken,
And stoop and build 'em up with worn-out tools;

If you can make one heap of all your winnings
And risk it on one turn of pitch-and-toss,
And lose, and start again at your beginnings
And never breathe a word about your loss;
If you can force your heart and nerve and sinew
To serve your turn long after they are gone,
And so hold on when there is nothing in you
Except the Will which says to them: "Hold on!"

If you can talk with crowds and keep your virtue,
Or walk with kings—nor lose the common touch,
If neither foes nor loving friends can hurt you,
If all men count with you, but none too much;
If you can fill the unforgiving minute
With sixty seconds' worth of distance run—
Yours is the Earth and everything that's in it,
And—which is more—you'll be a Man, my son!

                    Rudyard Kipling
            (December 30, 1865–January 18, 1936)

144

Love

Love gives naught but itself and takes
Naught but from itself.
Love possesses not nor would it be possessed;
For love is sufficient unto love.

Kahlil Gibran, The Prophet

Only when you drink from the river of silence shall you
   indeed sing.
And when you have reached the mountain top,
   then shall you begin to climb.
And when the earth shall claim your limbs, then shall you
   truly dance.

Kahlil Gibran, The Prophet

For what is it to die but to stand naked in the wind
   and to melt into the sun?

Kahlil Gibran, The Prophet

For life and death are one, even as the river and the sea are
one.

Kahlil Gibran, The Prophet

Most men lead lives of quiet desperation and go to the
   grave with the song still in them.

Henry David Thoreau, American Author

(1817–1862)

Additional Information

For more information on The Knights of Malta and
The Sovereign Order of St. John of Jerusalem
please visit: www.sosjmalta.org

For more information on the Lord Strathcona's Horse (Royal
Canadians)
please visit: www.strathconas.ca

For more information about Sergio Penha Brazilian Jiu Jitsu
please visit: www.sergiopenha.com

For more information about Sir Jason Winters
please visit: www.sirjasonwinters.com

FOR BOOK UPDATES AND ADDITIONAL BONUS MATERIAL PLEASE
VISIT:

www.sirjasonwinters.com/whatif.htm